Arden

Arden

A STUDY OF HIS PLAYS

by

ALBERT HUNT

EYRE METHUEN
LONDON

First published in Great Britain in 1974
by Eyre Methuen Ltd
11 New Fetter Lane, London EC4P 4EE
Copyright © 1974 Albert Hunt

Printed in Great Britain by
Butler & Tanner Ltd, Frome and London

SBN 413 28930 3 hardback
SBN 413 28940 0 paperback

Contents

Illustrations

b THE HAPPY HAVEN: original production by the Bristol Old Vic Company, 1960
(*Photo: Desmond Tripp*)

4a THE WORKHOUSE DONKEY: original production by Stuart Burge at Chichester, 1963; Frank Finlay (*Alderman Butterthwaite*)
(*Photo: Angus McBean, Harvard Theatre Collection*)

b THE BALLYGOMBEEN BEQUEST: production by Brian McAvera, in the Falls Road, Belfast, 1972
(*Photo: Brian McAvera*)

5 ARMSTRONG'S LAST GOODNIGHT: production by John Dexter and William Gaskill at the National Theatre, 1965; Albert Finney (*Johnny Armstrong*)
(*Photo: Angus McBean, Harvard Theatre Collection*)

6 THE HERO RISES UP: original production by John Arden and Margaretta D'Arcy at the Round House, 1968; Henry Woolfe (*Nelson*); Bettina Jonic (*Lady Hamilton*)
(*Photo: Donald Cooper*)

7a THE HERO RISES UP: production by Bill Hays and the Nottingham Playhouse Company at Edinburgh, 1969; Thelma Ruby (*Lady Emma Hamilton*); Robin Parkinson (*Nelson*)
(*Photo: Allan Hurst, courtesy of Nottingham Playhouse*)

b THE HERO RISES UP: production by John Arden and Margaretta D'Arcy at the Round House, 1968; Ann Mitchell (*Lady Nelson*); Henry Woolfe (*Nelson*); Bettina Jonic (*Lady Hamilton*)
(*Photo: Donald Cooper*)

8a THE ROYAL PARDON: original production by John Arden and Margaretta D'Arcy at the Beaford Arts Centre, 1966; John Arden (*Policeman*)
(*Photo: John Lane*)

b THE ROYAL PARDON: original production by John Arden and Margaretta D'Arcy at the Beaford Arts Centre (*Photo: John Lane*)

The photograph of John Arden on the front of the cover is by Roger Mayne and that of Albert Hunt on the back of the cover by David Sheard

Author's Note

This book is about the plays of John Arden. But no study of his work would be accurate without full acknowledgement of the part played by his wife, Margaretta D'Arcy.

From the beginning, Margaretta D'Arcy, a former professional actress, has contributed ideas and material and criticism and technical know-how to John Arden's work. In recent years she has increasingly shared in the actual writing.

Stylistically it is clumsy and irritating to keep referring to Arden/D'Arcy, and so, for convenience, I have usually referred to them, when writing of plays on which they have collaborated, as the Ardens. This is not intended to suggest in any way that Margaretta D'Arcy is less than an equal partner in the collaboration.

Of the earlier plays, *The Happy Haven* owed most to Margaretta D'Arcy. Although she did not actually write any of the play, she worked closely with Arden during the writing, and contributed many of the key ideas.

The following plays are, in every sense, collaborations:

> *The Business of Good Government*
> *The Royal Pardon*
> *Ars Longa, Vita Brevis*
> *The Hero Rises Up*
> *The Island of the Mighty*
> *The Ballygombeen Bequest*

Margaretta D'Arcy's influence on Arden's work has not been confined to offering ideas and collaborating on the writing. She has been the driving force behind the experiments in which he has been involved outside the professional theatre – particularly the Kirbymoorside Festival and, more recently, the work (in Oughterard) which led to *The Bally-gombeen Bequest*. Without her, as he himself puts it, he would have been a different, and a lesser, playwright.

John Arden

1930   Born in Barnsley, Yorkshire, on 26 October, son of C. A. Arden and A. E. Layland.

      Educated at Sedbergh School and went on to study architecture at King's College, Cambridge, and Edinburgh College of Art.

1955   Production of *All Fall Down* by fellow students at Edinburgh.

      Met Margaretta D'Arcy.

1956   Production of radio play *The Life of Man* – this won the BBC Northern Region prize.

1957   Production of *The Waters of Babylon* at the Royal Court, 20 October, director Graham Evans.

1958   *Soldier, Soldier* written for BBC Television.

      When is a Door not a Door? produced at the Embassy Theatre, Swiss Cottage, by the Central School of Drama, 2 June, director Robert Cartland.

      Production of *Live Like Pigs* by English Stage Society at the Royal Court, 30 September, directors George Devine and A. Page.

1959   Production of *Serjeant Musgrave's Dance* at the Royal Court, 22 October, director Lindsay Anderson.

1960   *Soldier, Soldier* presented on BBC Television, 16 February, director Stuart Burge.

      The Happy Haven at the Royal Court, 14 September, director William Gaskill.

      The Business of Good Government presented as the Christmas play at the Church of St Michael, Brent Knoll, Somerset, directed by the authors.

1961   Germany's first chance to sample Arden's work –
Serjeant Musgrave's Dance published by Rowohlt Verlag.
Wet Fish presented on BBC Television, 3 September,
director Peter Dews.

1962   First performance in the German language of *Serjeant
Musgrave's Dance* at Basle Stadttheater, Switzerland,
27 February, director Adolf Spalinger.
The Life of Man broadcast by Norddeutscher Rundfunk.
First performance in Germany of *Serjeant Musgrave's
Dance* at Das Jung Theater, Hamburg, 13 September,
director Viktor Warsitz.
Serjeant Musgrave's Dance on BBC Television.

1963   Production of *The Workhouse Donkey* at the Festival
Theatre, Chichester, 8 July, producer Stuart Burge.
Ironhand produced at the Bristol Old Vic, November,
director Val May.
Irish première of *The Happy Haven* at Gate Theatre,
Dublin, 2 December, director John Beary.

1964   *Armstrong's Last Goodnight* produced at the Glasgow
Citizens' Theatre, 5 May, director Denis Carey.
Production of *Ars Longa, Vita Brevis*, director Peter
Brook.

1965   *The Workhouse Donkey* produced at Göttingen, 20
February.
German première of *Ars Longa, Vita Brevis* at Munich,
27 March.
German translation of *Ars Longa* published in
Theater Heute, May.
German translation of *The Workhouse Donkey* published
in *Theater Heute*, June.
Production of *Left-Handed Liberty* at the Mermaid
Theatre, 14 June, director David Williams.
Armstrong's Last Goodnight produced at the Chichester
Festival Theatre, July, directors John Dexter and
William Gaskill.

Armstrong at the Old Vic with Albert Finney, 12 October.

Serjeant Musgrave's Dance produced by the English Stage Company at the Royal Court, 9 December, director Jane Howell.

1966   January – *Live Like Pigs* in rep. at the Glasgow Citizens' Theatre.

Serjeant Musgrave's Dance in rep. at the Royal Court from 31 January.

Serjeant Musgrave performed in Belgium and Holland.

March – *Armstrong's Last Goodnight* performed by the National Theatre at the Chichester Festival and at the Citizens' Theatre, Glasgow.

Production of *Friday's Hiding* at the Royal Lyceum Theatre, Edinburgh, 29 March, directors Sheila Ronald and Tom Fleming.

Armstrong's Last Goodnight produced at Bochum, Germany, 17 April, director Hans Schalla.

May – German translation of *Armstrong* published in *Theater Heute*.

8 August – *The Happy Haven* given American première at the Long Wharf Theater, New Haven.

The Royal Pardon performed at the Beaford Arts Centre, Devon, 1 September, directed by the authors.

October – Arden commissioned to write *The Island of the Mighty* for the Canon Studio Theatre.

German première of *Live Like Pigs* at Stuttgart, 4 November, director Peter Palitzsch.

December – German translation of *Live Like Pigs* published in *Theater Heute*.

1967   *Armstrong's Last Goodnight* produced in Basle, 24 February, director Ernst Kuhr.

The Workhouse Donkey presented at the Nottingham Playhouse, 25 October, director John Neville.

Live Like Pigs produced in Kiel, 14 November, director Helmet Gerg.

German première of *The Happy Haven* at Nuremberg, 9 December, director Konrad Höller.

Christmas – *The Royal Pardon* presented by the Unicorn Theatre Club at the New Arts Theatre.

1968   *Harold Muggins is a Martyr* produced at the Unity Theatre.

The True History of Squire Jonathan and his Unfortunate Treasure staged as a lunchtime performance by Interaction Theatrescope at the Ambiance Theatre, 17 June, director Ed Berman.

September – *The Happy Haven* produced in Holland.

Institute of Contemporary Arts presentation of *The Hero Rises Up* at the Round House, 6 November, directed by the authors.

December – *The Royal Pardon* at the Arts Theatre.

1969   *The Hero Rises Up* presented by the Nottingham Playhouse Company at the Edinburgh Festival, 8 September.

1970   First performance on BBC Radio of *The Bagman*.

1971   June – *The Hero Rises Up* in rep. at the Northcott Theatre, Exeter.

1972   First production of *The Ballygombeen Bequest*.

December – First production of *The Island of the Mighty* at the Aldwych Theatre; production disowned by John Arden and Margaretta D'Arcy.

I

Introduction

If one had asked of me my name
I freely could have told the same –
John Arden (thirty-eight) of ancient family,
Writer of plays for all the world to see,
To see, and pay for, and to denigrate:
Such was my work since 1958. . . .
    John Arden: *The Bagman* (1970)

(1)

From the beginning of his career as a playwright, John Arden
has been at the centre of controversy. His first professionally
staged play, *The Waters of Babylon*, was presented at the Royal
Court Theatre, London, for one experimental Sunday evening performance-without-décor in October 1957. 'It never
reached more than the one performance,' writes John Russell
Taylor, 'and was generally greeted with extreme puzzlement
if not outright hostility.'[1] His second play, *Live Like Pigs*,
was misunderstood even by the producers. Each scene is
introduced and presented by a ballad singer. The directors
never knew what to do with this man. He was, writes Arden,
'put on the stage between the scenes and quickly taken off
again so that no one was really clear whether he was in the
play or out of it'. In his suggestions 'to any producer

[1] John Russell Taylor: Introduction to *John Arden, Three Plays*,
Penguin 1967, p. 10.

interested in presenting *Live Like Pigs*', Arden feels he has to
include the sardonic hint, 'The play is in large part meant to
be funny.'[1]

Arden's third play, *Serjeant Musgrave's Dance*, is now
accepted as a masterpiece: it has become a prescribed text in
English Literature examinations. But its first performance,
in October 1959, was greeted with critical hostility. 'Another
dreadful ordeal,' wrote Harold Hobson; and the *New States-
man* critic commented, '. . . should have been a very good
play. But it isn't, despite seriousness, ambition, good situations and moments of stylish language.' By the time the
critics were beginning to realize that *Musgrave* was a very
good play, *The Happy Haven* had arrived, and was being
written off as a thin joke in bad taste – if only, it was suggested, Arden had written another *Musgrave*. . . .

This skirmishing between Arden and the critics has
continued through every play he has written. It reached a
climax in November 1968, when the critics arrived at the
Round House for the first night of *The Hero Rises Up*,
written and directed by Arden and his wife, Margaretta
D'Arcy, to find that their tickets were useless because the
Ardens had turned it into a free performance. 'While we were
producing the play,' writes Arden in his preface to the
published version, 'we became involved in a quarrel with
our management, the ICA . . . and as the audience assembled
we stood in the foyer like a pair of vexed Picts, committing
what in my childhood was the prime social crime of the lower
middle-class suburb where I lived – we were "Brawling on
the Doorstep" with the managerial representatives.' The
critics, fighting for places as if they were at a football match,
assumed that this chaos, in which many people could neither
see nor hear, represented the Ardens' latest idea of 'free
theatre': and Simon Trussler, in the *Tulane Drama Review*,

[1] Introductory Note to *Live Like Pigs* in *John Arden, Three Plays*
(Penguin), p. 101.

produced a homily about the conflict between the literary qualities of the play and the free-for-all of the situation. (In fact, the chaos was never intended: it was the result of a complete breakdown between authors and management – and a surprising and overwhelming public response. But the critics only saw it as confirmation of all they'd ever written about Arden's wilfulness and deliberate obscurantism.)

Moreover, the critics have not simply been content to express bafflement. They have invented – and then accepted – a reason for their own bewilderment. Why, asks John Russell Taylor in *Anger and After*, did *The Waters of Babylon* 'prove so difficult for its first audience?' 'The answer to that,' he goes on, 'is the key to the greater or lesser difficulties which audiences have found with all Arden's work: you never know where he stands in the play.'[1] And J. W. Lambert, introducing the Penguin text of *Live Like Pigs*, writes, 'But he too takes no sides.'

John Russell Taylor develops this argument in *Anger and After*. 'Arden permits himself in his treatment of the characters and situations in his plays to be less influenced by moral preconceptions than any other writer in the British theatre today.'[2] And he quotes Arden's reference to *Live Like Pigs* ('I approve outright neither of the Sawneys nor the Jacksons') in support of his statement that 'Arden's attitude to his creations is quite uncommitted.'

John Russell Taylor's statement is in direct contrast to the one made by Arden himself in his preface to his radio play, *The Bagman*, a preface written in 1971. Arden states:

> Mao Tsetung, that succinct poet, has said, 'Whatever the enemy opposes, we must support: whatever the enemy supports, we must oppose.' . . . I hope I have made it clear in *The Bagman* . . . that I recognize as the enemy the fed man, the clothed man,

[1] John Russell Taylor: Introduction to *John Arden, Three Plays* (Penguin), p. 10.
[2] John Russell Taylor, *Anger and After*, Methuen, London, 1962, p. 84.

the sheltered man, whose food, clothes and house are obtained
at the expense of the hunger, the nakedness, and the exposure of
so many millions of others: and who will allow anything to be
said, in books or on the stage, so long as the food, clothes, and
house remain undiminished in his possession.

In other words, Arden is asserting, and not for the first time,
the intensity of his commitment. Where, then, does this misunderstanding of his work spring from?

A clue is to be found in a letter Arden wrote to *Encore*[1]
about a review of *Armstrong's Last Goodnight* by Edwin
Morgan, which had appeared in the previous issue.[2] *Armstrong's Last Goodnight* tells the story of how Lindsay, a
cultured poet-diplomat in the service of James V of Scotland,
sets out to bring Johnnie Armstrong and his gang of
marauding, borderland outlaws, back into the King's service.
Lindsay is full of good intentions. He believes that law and
order can be established in a civilized, humane way, by the
exercise of diplomatic skills. And so he tries to woo Armstrong by offering him a royal pardon and making him a
petty overlord. Only this fails: and in the end Lindsay is
forced to betray Armstrong. He offers him a safe-conduct to
the King, and the King has him hanged.

Edwin Morgan begins by accepting the argument that
Arden refuses to take sides, and that therefore he has 'no
points to make'. The play's theme, he goes on, 'would
suggest a strong current of sympathy, perhaps even tragic . . .
directed towards Johnnie Armstrong. But – this is an Arden
play! Sympathy never develops very far. . . . We are never
asked to identify with this character, which indeed is presented very largely in a comic light. Conversely, we don't
find ourselves blaming Lindsay overmuch.' The play, Morgan
concludes, is about 'an expediency of which the author does
not visibly disapprove'.

[1] *Encore*, September–October 1964.
[2] *Encore*, July–August 1964

Morgan's conclusions tell us more about what he expects from a play than about *Armstrong's Last Goodnight*. He would like to be able to feel sympathy with a tragic hero whose actions he can admire. And he would like his moral indignation to be aroused by the actions of a man of whom he can, quite simply, disapprove. Above all, he wants to be able to identify himself with a character whose fate he can pity – as Brecht puts it, to be able to say, 'Yes, I have felt like that, too. Just like me. It's only natural.' Morgan is asking for a heroic tragedy, which will offer him a sense of catharsis. Arden's reply is categorical:

> I find the whole sequence of events in the play so alarming and hateful (and at the same time so typical of political activity at any period) that I have – perhaps rashly – taken for granted a similar feeling among the audience. If such a feeling does exist . . . then an over-emphasis upon it in the course of the play becomes re-dundant and self-defeating. My views on the Armstrong story are positive enough – Lindsay was wrong. . . I know I have not said this in so many words in the course of the play, but it was, I hoped, implied by my treating of the story and the persons in-volved in it. If this is not the case, then I have failed at the basic workman level of conveying to the audience the style and type of the entertainment they are faced with.[1]

But at this point we come to the heart of the misunder-standing between John Arden and his critics. John Arden's political position has always, it seems to me, been completely clear. He is a revolutionary, who instinctively and intellectu-ally rejects authority. As the political situation has changed and his own experience has widened, the emphasis on particular points of detail may have shifted. So, at the time of *Serjeant Musgrave's Dance*, he described himself as a pacifist who knew that if he was hit he would want to hit back; whereas after a visit to India, he indicates, in the preface to *The Bagman*, a dissatisfaction with the Ghandian politics of

[1] *Encore*, September–October 1964.

non-violence and a growing sympathy towards a Maoist form of violent revolutionary activity. But in all his work, he examines social institutions and social relationships from a revolutionary point of view.

This revolutionary attitude is embodied in 'the style and type of the entertainment' offered in his plays. At first sight, this style, verbal, apparently literary, seems to be acceptable enough to critics and audiences who have been taught to equate theatre with literature and seriousness with tragic feeling. But, on closer inspection, Arden turns out to be making demands on his audience which radically undermine the conventional responses that people bring to what Arden has called the 'legitimate' theatre.

The confusion between Arden and his critics springs basically from this fact: that they go to the theatre unconsciously expecting one 'style and type . . . of entertainment', and he offers them another. And this other style which he offers them happens to be one which rejects the basic assumptions the cultivated theatre-going public holds about what makes 'good' theatre.

(2)

And also I was, was I not, in a dream
Where women are always exactly what they seem
Instead of being no better than they are.
John Arden: *The Bagman* (1970)

The central unstated assumption that has dominated European theatre for more than a century is that, like the women in *The Bagman*, things 'are always exactly what they seem'.

Throughout theatre history, the question of stage illusion has always been discussed. But only in the naturalist European theatre of the nineteenth and twentieth centuries has it come to be taken for granted that illusion – what Samuel Johnson called 'the supposed necessity of making the drama credible' –

is the main object of any serious drama. This conviction is deeply rooted in the consciousness of those who shape the established British theatre. Even that bizarre, surrealist comedian, Marty Feldmann, when he was put into a *Wednesday Play*, was turned into a 'plausible character'.

At first sight, this devotion to illusion seems to have been challenged over the last fifty years. Every director or critic who has read Gordon Craig knows that naturalism has its limitations. But, in practice, a rejection of naturalism usually boils down to nothing more than a simplification of the scenery. The basic assumption of naturalist theatre – that the spectator must be convinced of the plausibility and reality of what he is seeing – is rarely seriously questioned.

This devotion to plausibility is most clearly seen in the attitude of directors, and more particularly actors, to the creation of 'character'. Characters, it is assumed, must be convincing as real people: they must always act 'in character'; their behaviour must be explicable. So, the cluttered scenery may have gone from *King Lear*, but the actor playing the King will still begin his work by assuming that it is his job to persuade the audience that they are seeing a real old man, and sharing in his misery; while it would never occur to the actor playing the part of the blind Gloucester that, at the moment of his leap from the imaginary cliff, part of the actor's vocabulary might be a somersault and a tumble.

Even in the avant-garde, 'experimental' theatre this unconscious commitment to illusion persists. For example, in the first part of Peter Brook's *US*, the actors presented an image of the Vietnam war, using all kinds of non-illusionist skills: but when, in the second act, we came to the 'meat' of the drama, the self-analysis of a middle-class intellectual girl, the scene only worked to the extent that Glenda Jackson was able to persuade the Aldwych audience that she *was* the character she was portraying – and to lure the audience into identifying themselves with her.

The question of identification is central to a theatre of
illusion. For illusion can only work to the extent that the
spectator's awareness of what is actually happening can be
broken down. If the illusion is successful, the spectator will
be persuaded to blot out that half of his mind that tells him
he is only seeing a play. And the simplest way of persuading
him to do this is to invite him to identify himself totally with
the character on the stage.

So, if the illusion in *Othello* is successful, the spectator, at
the moment when Othello is strangling Desdemona, is
identified with the tragic hero, is sharing his feelings of self-
pity: is much too close to him, in fact, to notice critically
that a wretched pun like, 'Put out the light and then put out
the light' is calling attention to the absurd, self-dramatizing
qualities of the central figure – is putting a question mark
against the very concept of a 'tragic hero'.

And this brings us to what is perhaps the most important
feature of the theatre of illusion – that it is essentially a theatre
of acceptance. It is a form of theatre that can only work by
persuading you to leave your critical, questioning faculties
outside, and allow yourself to be carried along by a tide of
emotion. So that when, for example, at the end of Arnold
Wesker's *Roots*, Beattie assures you that she's talking, you're
carried away by her excitement, moved by her joy. And you're
much too busy being moved to notice that what she is saying
is exactly what she's been saying all through the play, when
she's only been quoting her arty boy friend.

But if, in Arden's *Serjeant Musgrave's Dance*, you identify
yourself totally with Musgrave, the play becomes obscure –
which is why many critics found it, in the first place, confusing. Arden, however, has specifically rejected such attempts
at identification. In a *Peace News* interview in 1963 he
said:

> I don't understand this assumption that some people have that
> you have to present the audience with a character they can

identify with. I think you can identify with any character at any given moment of the play. I never write a scene so that the audience can identify with any particular character. I try and write the scene truthfully from the point of view of each individual character.[1]

But this takes us into a completely different tradition of theatre.

(3)

> My little people in a row
> Sit on the stage and watch the show
> The show they watch is rows and rows
> Of people watching them. Who knows
> Which is more alive than which?
>
> John Arden: *The Bagman* (1970)

Arden refers to this other tradition in the *Peace News* interview, when he describes a visit to a pantomime in Dublin:

> . . . an individual dressed as a gorilla bounded on to the stage and did a lot of knockabout with two comedians, and then came leaping off into the audience in a completely hideous gorilla costume, and raced about the audience, plonked himself down into a fat woman's lap and took her hat off, deposited her hat on a bald man, then flung its arms round another bald man and nuzzled him in the face. It was the most extraordinary thing I've ever seen in a theatre. . . . And just as you began to wonder how far it was going to go the gorilla suddenly bounded back on to the stage, unzipped the costume, and it was an attractive chorus girl in a little dress. And then everybody cheered and clapped. This sort of thing is acceptable in pantomime: people love it. But we haven't got round to taking our pleasures sufficiently casually in the legitimate theatre yet.[2]

[1] From 'A theatre of sexuality and poetry', an interview reported in *Peace News*, 30 August 1963 (reprinted in *Encore*, September–October 1965, 'On Comedy', p. 15.)

[2] *Peace News* interview, as cited above (in *Encore*, p. 17)

Compare such a scene with the theatre of illusion. The scene's success depends, in the first place, on the spectator being constantly aware that what he is seeing is *not* real. What he enjoys is the knowledge that there's an actor zipped up in the gorilla costume.

But at the same time, this fake gorilla impinges on the real world. The hats it takes off are real enough, and so is the embarrassment it causes. But the final satisfaction of the episode comes when you are presented with a surprising physical discovery. The suit is unzipped, and instead of the actor you know was there, out steps a pretty girl. Your sense of certainty and reality has been dislocated. (In the legitimate theatre, you would be complaining that the scene wasn't 'convincing'. What pretty girl would want to make herself look like a gorilla? Or, 'What does this reveal to me about her character?' you would ask.)

Instead of accepting illusion, the pantomime plays with it; and in doing so declares its attachment to a tradition that stretches back in English theatre beyond Shakespeare, and comes right forward to such comedians as Frankie Howerd and Morecambe and Wise.

In Shakespeare's theatre there's a constant playing with levels of reality. Sometimes, Shakespeare comments on the conventions directly, as in the play within the play of Bottom and the weavers, and Hamlet's speech to the Players. But elsewhere, he uses them with complete confidence, even at the height of an apparently tragic situation. Thus, Cleopatra, on the point of suicide, can say:

> I shall see
> Some squeaking Cleopatra boy my greatness
> I' the posture of a whore . . .

– the point being that the Elizabethan audience is consciously reminded, at an emotional peak in the play, that *this* Cleopatra is, in fact, also being played by a boy. And in *The Tempest* we have, as Tillyard points out, a masque 'executed by players pretending to be spirits, pretending to be real actors, pretending to be supposed goddesses and rustics'. At the end of the masque, Prospero, himself an actor, can say (of these real actors):

> These our actors
> As I foretold you, were all spirits and
> Are melted into air, into thin air.

It may seem a long way from the subtleties of Shakespeare to the deliberate crudities of Frankie Howerd or Morecambe and Wise, but the assault on illusion and the playing with different levels of reality is clearly part of the same tradition. So, Frankie Howerd, dressed up in the middle of an obviously fake Pompeii, will announce a dramatic prologue, and will break off to berate the audience for not laughing quickly enough at a gag ('I can't wait all night, you know'), or will complain about the crudity of the script; while Morecambe, playing in the high drama of *Mutiny on the Bounty*, will appear as Robert Newton playing Long John Silver, leaning on a crutch (he'll change legs from time to time) and carrying on his shoulder a ship's cat ('The parrot is in the cat'), which turns out to be made of cardboard and is attached to a cloak which he takes off.

John Arden's theatre is closer to the comedy of Morecambe and Wise than to the well-ordered world of, say, Terence Rattigan. In *The Waters of Babylon*, his first stage play, he consciously uses what he calls a provincial pantomime set – which is also the Morecambe and Wise set: curtains drawn, leaving a corridor at the front of the stage, on which actions can take place while scenes are changed. His hero, Krank, does a quick-change gag, going into a gent's lavatory as a brothel-keeper, and emerging as a respectable architect. *The Happy Haven* is built round a convention of old people being played by obviously young actors. And the climax of *The*

Royal Pardon comes when an actor pretending to be a policeman attacks, with a wooden sword, an actress pretending to
be a princess: only the policeman insists that the princess is
really a stage carpenter in disguise, and the princess complains that the obviously wooden sword is real. There's a
prince, too, wearing a cardboard crown, which makes a
clang when it falls to the floor. The policeman thought it was
only cardboard, he says . . .

In the theatre of illusion the central aim of writers, actors,
designers, directors is to convince the audience that everything is as it seems. It's a theatre of persuasion. But the
theatre of 'the popular dramatic tradition' has precisely the
opposite aim: to question appearances. Be careful: that
object you expect to be a parrot may turn out to be a cat,
and the cat may be a cut-out. That cardboard crown may
clang when it's dropped: which are you to believe, your eyes
or your ears?

The theatre of illusion is a theatre of persuasion. Arden's
theatre, like Shakespeare's – like Brecht's – is a theatre of
scepticism and questioning.

> Closely observe the behaviour of these people:
> Consider it strange, although familiar,
> Hard to explain, although the custom,
> Hard to accept, though no exception.
> Even the simplest action, apparently simple,
> Observe with mistrust. . . .
> Bertolt Brecht: *The Exception and the Rule*

(4)

> My little men, though made of wood,
> Can frame a gesture just as good.
> Laugh and leap and shake with terror,
> My little men will be your mirror.

What you do or what you did
From little people can't be hid:
They will know it and reflect
In strut and jerk your every act. . . .
John Arden: *The Bagman* (1970)

If John Arden has been drawn towards a theatre in which a
crown can be both cardboard and can yet make a clang when
it falls, it's not out of a sentimental desire to revive a folksy
tradition (he's made his own comment on that kind of
folksiness in *The Hero Rises Up*). It's because, ideologically as
well as temperamentally, he sees this form of theatre as a
mirror of the world he is trying to portray.

That theatre is, in its *form*, a reflection of an ideological
attitude is a concept that many people find difficult to grasp.
The usual assumption is that a play's 'message' is carried
by the character with whom the spectator is invited to
identify – so that, for example, the 'message' of John
Osborne's *Look Back In Anger* is to be found in Jimmy
Porter's outbursts against society. But *Look Back In Anger*
isn't simply a vehicle for Jimmy Porter. In its form it reflects
Osborne's preoccupations – which are more to do with
feelings than with actions, with intentions rather than events.

The ideology of the theatre of illusion is that of nineteenth-
century rationalism, what the American critic Lionel Trilling
has called, 'the liberal imagination'. 'It is one of the tendencies
of liberalism,' writes Trilling, 'to simplify, and this tendency
is natural in view of the effort which liberalism makes to
organize the elements of life in a rational way.'[1] The theatre
of illusion thrives on simplification.

The theatre of illusion, for example, takes the appearance
for the reality. This is what people look like; this is how
they talk. Therefore, this is what they are. They're pinned
down, labelled, categorized. By the end of the play, we think
we understand them.

[1] *The Liberal Imagination*, Secker & Warburg 1955, p. xiv.

Moreover, the theatre of illusion demands a reality that is basically static. If you're carefully constructing an illusion of reality, you can't suddenly kick that illusion to pieces and suggest that reality might be totally different. Shakespeare can put into the mouth of a blunt Roman soldier a speech beginning, 'The barge she sat in, like a burnished throne / Burned on the water . . .'[1] because what matters to him at that point is not making Enorbabus 'convincing', but giving a picture of Cleopatra. But in a naturalist play, the prime demand is for 'consistency', a consistency that allows us to pin a character down in rational terms. A man tells a joke; we laugh, but we also make a mental note – the man is a joker. We have cornered this little bit of him; we know where we are. And soon, to confirm the consistency, the dramatist will give him another joke. We are in the world of the graven image, in which we see a person entirely in terms of the label we can fix on to him. Naturalist theatre is the theatre of the graven image. (In Olivier's film of *Hamlet*, Hamlet himself becomes simply 'the man who could not make up his mind' – a completely naturalist conception.)

Ideologically, the theatre of illusion has another effect: the narrowing down of social processes to the world of individual feelings. Since we're asked to accept that reality is what we see, and since what we see is people offering a plausible imitation of how the characters they are playing would behave in 'real life', the reality of, say, the firestorm in Hamburg, is narrowed down, in Hochhuth's play *Soldiers*, to the expression on Churchill's face when he's shown the photographs of the damage. The emphasis is focussed not on the actual raid, but on what the actor can show us of Churchill's feelings. (Churchill is, of course, distressed. We're moved by his distress. Still, we tell ourselves, that's the burden great men have to bear in wartime. We're never actually shown the content of the photographs that distress

[1] *Antony and Cleopatra*, Act II, Scene 3.

him.) Similarly, in Günter Grass's *The Plebeians Rehearse the Uprising* (a play supposedly about how Brecht behaved during the East Berlin rising of June 1956), we're in fact shown very little of what happened during the rising (was it justified or not? what did Brecht actually do? should he have acted like that?). Instead, we're confronted, at the end, with an actor pouring out his guilt, and inviting us to share his feelings. ('You . . . you poor babes in the woods. Bowed down with guilt, I accuse you.') The theatre of illusion turns attention away from events and towards feelings. We experience a catharsis, and leave the theatre feeling luxuriously guilty.

Ideologically, therefore, the theatre of illusion offers a simplified view of life; technically, it tries to persuade the spectator to accept this simplified view as the whole of reality; and in this process of persuasion it asks the spectator to leave his critical imagination outside, and to lose himself, instead, in sympathetic feelings.

If Arden turns away from such a theatre, it's not out of any desire to be 'experimental', but because the form of the theatre of illusion can't contain his response to experience. In contrast to the theatre of illusion's simplified view of life, Arden's response is built on an intense awareness of contradictions, of the existence of opposites in any given situation. It's a dialectical view.

But the dialectic is expressed, not in terms of abstract, theoretical arguments – but of a concrete form of theatre in which a cardboard crown makes a clang when it falls to the floor – and in which a gorilla turns out to be a chorus girl in a little dress.

(5)

'In my view the Professor is a young man to be encouraged: though of course we must be careful.'

'We can encourage him by all means. And control him.'
'Not control. Suggest directions.'

John Arden: *The Bagman* (1970)

Arden, therefore, is working in a popular tradition, because
that tradition embodies his response to experience. But it's
a tradition that has almost disappeared in the medium in
which he works – the legitimate theatre – although, ironically, it has been preserved and developed in the new technological media (film and television) which reach popular
audiences far larger than Shakespeare could ever have
imagined. And these media have, in turn, helped to shape
the form of Arden's theatre.

The most obvious form in which the popular tradition is
preserved in the new media is the slapstick comedy. S. L.
Bethell, points out that 'criticism is usually levelled at slapstick in serious films, much as neo-classical criticism objects
to the mixture of comedy and tragedy in Shakespeare'.[1]
Arden doesn't hesitate to throw slapstick into the most
apparently solemn situations – the most striking example,
perhaps, being the latest, the custard pie fight with which
he and Margaretta D'Arcy end their play about Ireland, *The
Ballygombeen Bequest*.

But slapstick comedy is not the only form in which the
cinema and television have preserved elements of the popular
tradition. The mainstream Hollywood movie, with its
familiar stories, familiar settings, and, above all, familiar
stars, succeeded, over many generations, in 'conveying to the
audience the style and type of entertainment they are faced
with', and, in the process, created a far wider vocabulary
than the one usually acknowledged in grammars of the film.

This vocabulary has largely been built around the audience's
response to well-known stars. A writer or director handling,
for example, John Wayne or Frank Sinatra, or Richard

[1] S. L. Bethell, *Shakespeare and the Popular Dramatic Tradition*, Staples
Press 1944, p. 28.

Widmark, can assume that the audience will have a predictable response. There's a built-in alienation effect: John
Wayne is not simply the character he is playing, but also the
John Wayne one has seen in countless other films, and who
has a well-known persona off screen as well, which also
affects the audience's responses. So, in a film like *Red River*,
Howard Hawks can build his whole story round the assumption that the audience will identify John Wayne as the hero –
only to discover, as the film progresses, that Wayne has
gradually changed from hero into enemy.

Arden's theatre, at times, demands such a vocabulary.
Musgrave, in *Serjeant Musgrave's Dance*, resembles the John
Wayne character in *Red River*. At first, he seems to be the
hero: later, his actions are shown in a questionable light. But
whereas Hawks had Wayne, and could begin by taking the
audience's response for granted, Arden has to try and teach
his audience how to respond to Musgrave. In the theatre,
the common language Hawks could depend on doesn't
exist – which, again, helps to explain some of the confusions
surrounding the play's first reception.

Throughout his work Arden uses an idiom that would be
acceptable in pantomime, or in Hollywood, or in television
comedy, but which, in the 'legitimate' theatre seems strange
and incomprehensible. Why, then, hasn't Arden abandoned
a medium which is so clearly committed to an ideology he
doesn't share, and worked in the new, technological media
which seem closer to his 'type of entertainment'?

The answer lies partly in the structure of the film and
television industries. Television has, in the past, seriously
distorted his work. In writing about the television production
of *Wet Fish*, Arden refers to 'the intolerable situation that
our television networks have prepared for authors who get
above themselves. . . . When *Wet Fish* was presented . . . my
notions of the style of presentation were not consulted.'[1]

[1] Arden, Preface to *Soldier, Soldier and other plays*.

B

And when, in 1964, he wrote a script for the film version of
Ned Kelly, it was simply bought up by one of the major
companies, and never used.

But there seems to me to be a more fundamental reason why
Arden has continued to involve himself in theatre rather than
in the mass media. Both he and Margaretta D'Arcy see the
theatre as a place where, physically, people can share a particular experience in a particular way. Since 1960, experiments in
creating forms of theatre outside the established professional
framework have been an integral part of their work. Often
these experiments have grown simply out of the fact that they
were professional playwrights, driven by economic necessity
to live in out-of-the-way rural areas; and that, while living in
these places, they wanted to go on practising their profession.
But nowhere have they launched an activity without the
demand coming from the people amongst whom they were
living, or for whom the event was to be created. So in Brent
Knoll, in Somerset, they responded to a request by the vicar
for a nativity play, and worked with his parishioners on producing one; at Kirbymoorside, faced with a complete absence
of local entertainment, they created, around the cottage where
they lived, a month-long festival of anarchy. Later, with
students, they made a play for children at the request of the
Beaford Festival in Devon. In New York they staged a day-
long event about the Vietnam war, at the request of students
of New York University. And with the small farmers of
Oughterard, in County Galway, they made a film about the
incursions of the tourist industry.

To the Ardens this work is at least as important as the
staging of a new play at the Aldwych. But it is not separate
from their work in the professional theatre. It arises out of the
same concerns.

In analysing the Ardens' plays, we need to be aware that
they have been written in the context of a continuous struggle
to create new working relationships, both inside and outside

the professional theatre. And this struggle, too, is part of Arden's commitment – a commitment that many of his critics have insisted that he has never had.

2

Seven Plays for Professionals

ONE: THE WATERS OF BABYLON

The first of Arden's plays to be performed professionally in the London theatre was *The Waters of Babylon*. It was given one Sunday-night production-without-décor at the Royal Court Theatre in October 1957. At that time, the Royal Court, under George Devine, was giving a new impetus to British drama, first by having persuaded a number of established novelists to write for the theatre, and secondly by having discovered *Look Back In Anger*. Set in a Midlands bed-sitting room, and full of angry tirades against the establishment, John Osborne's play was seen partly as a protest against British society, but partly, too, as a reaction against the artificiality of British theatre. Two years later, the Royal Court's big success would be *Roots*, the play in which Arnold Wesker, with tape-recorder accuracy, reproduces the surface reality of life in a Norfolk cottage.

In contrast, *The Waters of Babylon* is a deliberately artificial play. Beginning with a music-hall comedian-type chat to the audience, it includes pantomime gags, songs, dances and verse monologues. One of the central characters, Conor

Cassidy, is a stage Irishman, and Arden actually calls attention to the fact. 'What part are you after playing these last five years,' Cassidy cries at one point when he discovers that his sister is a tart (he, of course, is a pimp), 'but sorrow and trouble upon the grey heads of them that has loved you.' 'Oh take him away,' says his sister, Teresa. 'The minute he sees me he thinks he's on the stage of the Abbey Theatre.'

The Waters of Babylon plays with staginess. It tells the story of a Polish émigré, Krank, who leads a double life. In the daytime he is the respectable assistant of an architect called Barbara Baulkfast: but at night he runs a lodging-house-cum-brothel. Another Polish émigré, Paul, to whom he owes five hundred pounds, tries to blackmail him into helping to blow up Bulganin and Krushchev during their visit to London. In an effort to raise the five hundred pounds and so buy himself out of the plot, Krank involves himself with a Premium Bond swindle, organized by a former Yorkshire town councillor, Charles Butterthwaite, a 'Napoleon of Local Government'. But the scheme goes wrong, and, in a sequence of accidents, Paul shoots Krank by mistake. As Krank lies dead, Butterthwaite leads everybody in the singing of a round, to the tune of 'The Ash Grove':

> We're all down in t'cellar-hoyle,
> Wi't'muck-slaghts on t'windows.

The first point that's striking about *The Waters of Babylon* is the intricacy of the story. In *Look Back In Anger*, for example, what happens is that one girl moves out, another moves in, and then the first girl comes back after having had a miscarriage. The story is very slight: the real content of the play lies in the exploration of a basically static situation. But in *The Waters of Babylon* the story turns and twists with every scene. And the details are put together with architectural precision. For example, in one of the early scenes, Krank complains that one of his girls, Bathsheba, hasn't brought his *Daily Mirror*. Later, it's through the *Daily Mirror* that we learn of the Russians' visit to London. Arden slips the detail casually and easily into place.

The complex story is, in fact, put together with great narrative skill. The scene, for instance, in which we first hear of the plot to blow up the Russians is pure Hitchcock. Krank and Barbara are in the middle of a lovers' tiff, when Paul arrives and introduces himself with a gag line: 'I am from the Holocaust Heating and Engineering Company. Always trusting to meet your every requirement.' While Barbara is out of the room, Paul, hammily, announces his intention of blowing up the Russian leaders. But in Barbara's presence, Krank and Paul discuss the relative merits of gas and oil heating. Over the phone, Barbara talks to the head-mistress of a junior school about the colour scheme of a classroom. Paul leaves with the same gag: 'Always trusting to meet your every requirement.'

The scene is built round the tension between the everyday work of an architect's office, and the plot to blow up Krushchev. It's full of double meanings and private games, and self-consciously melodramatic poses. And it's compli-cated by the fanaticism of Barbara's personal obsession with Krank. Some day, she says, one of his women will finish him. 'Oh, I don't imagine that is very likely,' says Krank – but in the end she is directly involved with Krank's acci-dental death. In an Arden play, the unimaginable becomes real, while the everyday looks unimaginably absurd.

There's a similar tightness about the scene at the climax of the play in which the Premium Bond ticket is drawn. The audience is first of all let into the plot: the tickets will be whirled in a drum; when the cymbals are clashed, Cassidy will put the lights out; in the darkness, Butterthwaite will give the winning ticket to Bathsheba, who is conducting the draw; the winning number will be held by Cassidy's sister, Teresa.

Once in the know, all the audience has to do is sit back and watch the scheme go wrong. A stock comic policeman establishes himself on the platform – his wife holds a ticket. 'Of course,' he says, 'if I was to win . . . They'd call it Evidence of Criminal Collusion—laugh. Oh there's a lot of funny jokers in the force.' Butterthwaite crawls out drunk, and dressed as Napoleon, from under the table, divides the audience into three parts, inciting them to shout, 'Austria, Prussia, Russia', and is on the point of encouraging them with a clash of cymbals, when he remembers the signal. Krank accidentally knocks the cymbals on the floor, and Cassidy puts the lights out. In the darkness, Butterthwaite can be heard saying, 'I tell you I've lost it.' When the lights go on again, Krank and Bathsheba are kneeling amongst a pile of tickets. The policeman advances towards them. 'Waterloo,' says Butterthwaite. When the ticket is drawn, it is, of course, the one belonging to the policeman's wife.

This intricate narrative is very precisely put together. But alongside this precision, the play has another structure, which gives the impression of being loose and episodic. It's a pantomime structure – even the set is that of a traditional pantomime, with curtains that draw to allow scene changes, in front of which linking scenes can be played – which takes the form of a series of music-hall turns.

So, the play opens with Krank chatting directly to the audience, like a music-hall compère. Later, the scene stops while he sings a song. Later still, there's a quick-change gag, as he goes into the lavatory at Baker Street underground as a lodging-house keeper, and comes out as an architects' assistant. Later still, Bathsheba and the black councillor, Joe Caligula, interrupt the action with a scene that is part dance, part ritual, part children's game and part Cole Porter:

> 'Say you was the railing and I was the park:'
> 'I am the lantern.'
> 'I'm all the dark.'

These apparent digressions work on their own terms: they're funny or entertaining in their own right. But through them, Arden carries the central ideas of the play.

For example, Krank's opening speech works on a number of levels. In the first place, it establishes a relationship with the audience. By talking to the audience, directly, as in music-hall, Krank breaks immediately out of the naturalist framework which pretends that the audience doesn't exist. Krank invites the audience to make contact with him, in the way that a music-hall audience would make contact with a comedian.

Secondly, the speech gives us information:

> Half-past seven of a morning . . . Cold, I think, yes, cold, rainy, foggy, perhaps by dinnertime it will snow. No? Perhaps not snow, it is after all spring. March, April, May, even in London, I do not think – even in North London, perhaps, not snow . . . That's the electric train. It goes past. . . .

By using the method of direct speech, Arden is able to set the scene very quickly, in a few lines.

Thirdly, the speech introduces us to a character. He's a man who is disarmingly open about himself. 'Why don't I wash my cups and plates more often than only once a week?' he asks. ''Cause I am a man of filthy habits in my house, is why.' We feel we ought to object to him. But in fact he's quite engaging. 'What is the matter with this salami?' he asks. 'I think, somebody, they've dropped it on the floor. It would disgust a drain-layer. But not me. For me, breakfast is to be enjoyed.' 'He enjoys it,' say the stage directions. Already, Arden is setting up in the audience a complex response to this man: his habits are clearly to be condemned – but he performs them with great charm.

Finally, since the speech is delivered by an alien, a man with a slight foreign accent, Arden is imposing on the audience an alien way of looking at the familiar. His reference

to London – 'even in North London' – gives a slightly
farcical twist to London geography: and his description of
an Irishman, Conor Cassidy, as 'another foreign man lives
in this London' slyly questions the way English people
normally think about Irishmen. In this opening speech,
Arden is adopting the Brechtian technique of making the
familiar seem strange.

The song with which Arden later breaks the narrative
surface of these opening scenes adds to the strangeness.
Bathsheba calls it Krank's dolorous song: Krank calls it
'The true story . . . of the life of me, of Krank. This was myself, you see, at an altogether different time of the world'. The
song is very beautiful, and has the feeling of a folk song:

> As I went down by Belsen town
> I saw my mother there
> She said, go by, go by my son, go by,
> But leave with me here
> Your lovely yellow hair.

> As I went down by Auschwitz town
> My brother looked out of the wall
> He said, go by, go by my brother, go by
> But leave with me here
> The lovely strong tooth from your skull.

> As I went down by Buchenwald town
> And there for my sweetheart I sought
> But she whispered, go by, Oh my darling go by
> You leave with me here
> The lovely red blood of your heart.

In the music-hall structure, the song comes at the moment
when the comedian would announce a sentimental number
to round off the turn. And the words are nostalgic, with the
repetitive form, and the folk imagery: yellow hair, red blood.
But the content of the song collides harshly with the tone.
The references to Belsen, Auschwitz, Buchenwald throw the

nostalgia into sharp, ironic relief. The song is disturbing in its irony – but Bathsheba suddenly makes the unthinkable normal again. 'Man,' she says, 'you must have travelled wide.'

Arden uses the idea of a music-hall song to introduce a new dimension to our understanding of Krank: the night-mare of Buchenwald is brought into the pantomime picture of a lodging–house in North London. And, later, Arden uses a quick-change gag – brothel-keeper to architect's assistant – as a peg on which to hang a philosophical state-ment. As Krank emerges transformed from the Baker Street lavatory, he says to the audience:

> I am a man of no one condition having no more country, no place, time, action, no social soul. I am easy and able to choose whatever alien figure I shall cut, where and wherever I am, in London: not any place in London but all places of London, for all of it and none of it is mine.

Here, Arden is making explicit the link between the *style* of the play, with its pantomime gags, and an attitude to experi-ence. Krank plays different roles, just as the pantomime comedian becomes different people by changing his clothes. Arden emphasizes the theatricality and role-playing by suddenly stepping back from the statement he has just made. 'Central European paradox,' comments Krank, in brackets.

Perhaps the most important stylistic device Arden uses as an apparent digression from the tight, narrative structure is that of having a character present himself directly, in form-alized speech, to the audience. In terms of the music-hall structure, these formalized speeches work as variety turns – monologues. But in terms of the narrative, they have the effect of forcing us to question our own preconceptions about how we might expect the characters to behave.

The first of these monologues occurs when Charlie Butterthwaite is introduced. After a few lines of dialogue, we are sure we know where we are with him. He's one of those blunt, successful northerners we've seen in countless plays and films from *Hobson's Choice* to *Room at the Top*. He will always call a spade a spade in an aggressively regional accent.

But, suddenly, in answer to the question, 'What is your profession?' Butterthwaite steps out of character to give a formalized account of his own career. The language is sharp and precise:

As a young lad I began in Trades Union offices.
Railways, smoke, black steel, canals, black stone.
That were my town, and where sets the power?
Mill owners: I saw that. Hundredweights of them.
Murky money. But not for me, not for our Charlie.
Conjure up the adverse power from out the crowded smoke.
Union Headquarters. Only a young lad: I begin: I go on:
From Union on to Council, Councillor to Alderman,
Alderman to Mayor, unfolded power of scarlet
broadening back and belly: but that weren't the secret:
it's not gold chain nor scarlet carries right power.
Committees, Chairman of this one, Secretary of that one,
Housing Development, Chamber of Trade,
Municipal Transport, Hospitals, Welfare Amenities
Eat your Christmas Dinners in the Lunatic Asylum,
Colliery Canteens, in the poor old Borough Orphanage,
Weekly photo in the paper in a paper hat and all
Cheery Charlie Butterthwaite: there was puddings to them
    dinners.

'The dialogue,' Arden once wrote in *Encore*, 'can be naturalistic and "plotty" as long as the basic poetic issue has not been crystallized. But when this point has been reached, the language becomes formal.'[1] Here, the poetic issue *has* been crystallized. Butterthwaite's speech is as much out of character as Enobarbus's description of Cleopatra on the

[1] *Encore*, May–June 1960, 'Telling a True Tale', p. 25.

barge: and it serves a similar function – it draws attention away from a private psychology, and towards an objectively describable situation.

The speech is economical: the town is conjured up in one line ('Railways, smoke, black steel, canals, black stone') and the power of the mill owners is summed up in the one word, 'Hundredweights'. In other words, they press down on the town like a dead weight. But against their 'murky money' Butterthwaite conjures up an 'adverse power' – the image is that of a necromancer. The speech then leads us up a false trail – to the scarlet and gold of the mayor, only to bring us in the end to the real power – 'Committees'. And alongside committees, demagoguery: 'Weekly photo in the paper in a paper hat'. But the personal ambition, the committee management and the publicity all point towards Butterthwaite's real social achievement: 'there was puddings to them dinners.'

What Arden has given us in this concise speech is a cool, objective picture of how private ambition is interwoven with social processes. Butterthwaite holds himself up for our inspection, without apology or explanation. This, says Arden, is how your society works. What do you think of it?

If Arden uses the monologue to force us to make a judgement about Butterthwaite and the society to which he belongs, he uses it even more strongly to make us look again at the central figure of the play – Krank himself. From the beginning of the play, there has been a contradiction between the way we feel we *ought* to react to Krank, and the reaction he in fact evokes. Thus, when we know he is a Rachmann-type exploiter, we would expect to be able to make an easy moral judgement about his activities. But the way in which he describes these activities and his charming *manner* disarms all our moral judgements:

A well-conducted lodging-house. I have eighty people in it. . . .
Thirty shillings a week one room, one bed, I provide packing-

cases if they wish to make any additional furniture. . . . Also I charge extra if a lodger wishes a guest for the night. I don't see, why is not that legitimate? But yet . . . they *will* talk about a disorderly house.

Moreover, we are told that he has been an inmate of Buchenwald, and there, too, is a moral paradox: that a victim should turn out to be an exploiter.

But towards the end of the play, we discover that Krank has not, in the conventional sense, been a victim of Buchenwald. The loyal Englishman, Henry Ginger ('Though the fool policeman sleeps, Henry Ginger wakes and creeps') has discovered that Krank was not an inmate but a guard. Paul, in despair, cries, 'I *must* understand this' – and Krank offers his own formalized explanation:

> You know, there's nothing difficult, psychological, obscure.
> It's a most easy story, not very long. I will tell you.
> 1939, my part of Poland is invaded by the Russians,
> So I find it convenient to join the Russian Army.
> I clean the officers' boots. Amusing. Then, 1941.
> My part of the Russian Army is destroyed by the Germans.
> So I find it convenient – so, once again, I find. . . .
> I clean the officers' boots. Amusing? I did not ask
> To be posted to Buchenwald.

The speech describes a process in matter-of-fact terms. The horror of Buchenwald becomes a matter of cleaning officers' boots. Krank, like Butterthwaite, offers himself for inspection. At the end of the speech, he asks:

> In Buchenwald was I prisoner, was I convenient soldier . . .
> So many thousands of people all lost in that cold field.
> Who knows what I was?

'We know what you were,' Paul replies – but at this point we are brought to the heart of the play. For *The Waters of Babylon* is precisely about the difficulty of knowing who people are, and of making obvious judgements. Are we involved, asks Arden, with tragedy or farce: with play-acting or truth: with games or reality? And is it possible to separate these categories? Aren't Belsen, and Buchenwald, and sexual jealousies, and Premium Bond swindles, and assassinations of politicians, and the holocaust all part of the same unreal drama, that happens to be real? (What, in fact, could have been more unbelievable and melodramatic than the assassination of John Kennedy, followed by the even more unbelievable killing of his brother Robert?) *The Waters of Babylon* asserts, through its *form*, that ordinary, everyday reality is unimaginably melodramatic, that farce is basically tragic, and that tragedy is only farce.

At the end of the play, Krank is shot, accidentally. Paul had been aiming at Henry Ginger, whom he imagines has stolen his bomb – though, in fact, the bomb has been taken by Cassidy for the use of the IRA. So Krank is killed by mistake. And at this point, the apparent contradiction between the tragic story and the farcical tone is crystallized. As Krank dies, he makes a cool, formal statement, in rhymed couplets:

> I said I was not going to die;
> Truth? I am afraid, I think it was a lie.
> So, only a few minutes to live,
> I must see can I not give
> Some clearer conclusion to this play
> To order your lives the neatest way . . .

The speech is jaunty and ironic. It once again deliberately destroys the dramatic illusion, reminding us that we are only seeing a play: and it puts into the mouth of a disordered, untidy man a statement about the imagined neatness of life. Confidently, Krank disposes of all the characters. Then he announces:

> I'm going to declare my identity at last.
> Place and time, and purposes,

Are now to be chosen for me.
I cannot any longer do without knowing them . . .
So many thousands of people
In a so large a cold field.
How did they get into it?
And what do they expect to find?

And he dies.

So that the 'clearer conclusion' turns out to be one more question mark. We don't, in the end, know Krank's identity, and the play denies us the right to pin him down in this way. All we can judge are his actions: and, as we judge them, Arden invites us, implicitly, to judge our own.

The Waters of Babylon is, ultimately, a play about the impossibility of making generalized moral statements. It invites us to examine specific concrete situations, to judge actions rather than identities. And it does so while telling an intricate and surprising story in the form of a series of music-hall turns.

TWO: LIVE LIKE PIGS

After the formal and narrative complexities of *The Waters of Babylon*, Arden's next play, *Live Like Pigs*, seems an altogether much more straightforward affair. 'When I wrote this play', Arden has said, 'I intended it to be not so much a social document as a study of differing ways of life brought sharply into conflict and both losing their own particular virtues under the stress of intolerance and misunderstanding. In others words, I was more concerned with the "poetic" than the "journalistic" structure of the play.'[1] But of all Arden's plays, *Live Like Pigs* is, at first sight, the closest to a 'social document'. Set in 'A post-war Council Estate in a north-country industrial town', it deals with an obvious social

[1] Introductory Note to *Live Like Pigs* in *John Arden, Three Plays*, Penguin, 1967.

problem: what happens when you forcibly put a group of gypsies into a council house. Moreover, the more noticeable non-naturalistic devices of *The Waters of Babylon* – the direct speeches to the audience, the sudden changes of texture, the passages of formal poetry – have disappeared. The only immediately apparent break from naturalism is to be found in the songs, and particularly in the ballad which introduces each scene. But in the original Royal Court production this ballad didn't work anyway. The play was, in fact, handled as one more example of a slice of working-class life – and one in which Arden had evaded the central problem of making working-class speech dramatic by creating a family of lyrical romanies.

Live Like Pigs, then, can be seen as a naturalistic social problem play, tarted up with songs and over-lyrical dialogue. But to see it in this way is to miss completely what Arden calls the 'poetic structure'.

Live Like Pigs tells the story of what happens when a family of gypsies, the Sawneys, is put into a council house next door to a would-be respectable family, the Jacksons. The Sawneys attract a much more extreme group of romanies, one of whom howls in the street at night: and eventually the 'respectable' neighbours are themselves roused to violence. At the end of the play, the police have to rescue the lawless gypsies from the fury of law-abiding householders.

This story seems to be presented in a series of naturalistic episodes. But the naturalism is more apparent than real. Take, for example, this passage from the opening scene.

> SAILOR *and* COL *come in through the front door pushing a home-made barrow consisting of a packing-case mounted on pram wheels. It is loaded with a great pile of household junk, topped by a chamber-pot and an old-fashioned horn gramophone. They also both carry bundles . . .*
>
> SAILOR. Two men to pull the barrow, one man pulls the barrow, one man walks beside it, that's *his* way.

COL. Ah, hold your gob, will you, I'm leading as much of the
   weight as you –

SAILOR. One man to pull it, one man to walk beside – it's the
   strong lad, he walks beside; the old man, he has to pull; that's
   his way. (*He sees the* OFFICIAL.) Who's this?

COL. All the road up from the back bottom of the hill, he's
   carrying-on. Why don't I smash his face for him? (*Sees the*
   OFFICIAL.) Who's this?

OFFICIAL. Mr Sawney? I'm from the Corporation.

The scene can be read as a not very accurate attempt to
reproduce working-class speech. But in fact it's taken
straight from music-hall. It belongs to the tradition that was
later to give birth to Steptoe and his son. The two men walk
on with a set of music-hall props – a packing-case on pram
wheels, junk, and a horn gramophone mixed up with a
chamber-pot. The props are 'naturalistic' in the sense that
they could convincingly belong to a family of gypsies: but
they also belong to that seaside comic-postcard tradition in
which a chamber-pot in itself can be relied on for a laugh.
(It would be possible to emphasize the gag by having the
old man struggle with the barrow, with the young man not
helping at all.)

The dialogue, too, belongs to the music-hall. There's the
repetitive patter ('Two men to pull the barrow, one man
pulls the barrow . . .'), the grumbles, made partly to each
other and partly in asides, the appeals to the audience, as in
pantomime ('That's *his* way.' 'Why don't I smash his face
for him?'). And there's a classic double-take: 'Who's this? . . .
Who's this?' The Official is the straight man, the fall guy.
'I'm from the Corporation,' he says pompously – and the
attempt at dignity makes him ridiculous in the context of
the packing-case and the chamber-pot.

If this scene is presented as an attempt to create an illusion
of what it's like to move into a council house in Barnsley,
then it simply becomes a glum, bad-tempered altercation

between two not very likeable people. The Official is no more than a crude caricature: and Sailor's song at the end of the scene ('Oh when I was a young strong man / I wandered on the sea . . .') is an irrelevant intrusion.

But if it's presented as a piece of music-hall, then everything becomes gay and acceptable. The mutual insults are part of a recognized tradition (to which, for example, Laurel and Hardy belong), the caricature official is *welcomed* as a caricature – and Sailor's song is expected: because comic scenes in music-hall always end with sentimental, nostalgic songs.

The play is, in fact, built round a series of music-hall sketches. A neighbour comes in for a bit of Coronation Street gossip, but Sailor frightens her away: 'Chase that bloody cow out o' here, and get me a sup o' tea.' A girl forgets her doorkey ('I've done ever such a soft thing'), and while she's waiting to get in is dated by a boy who plays, on his horn gramophone, 'Cigareets and whisky and wild, wild women'. A comic boaster goes to bed with a tart and get's more than he's bargained for. And there's the Old Croaker, with her catch-phrase, 'I tear them all up'.

Arden uses this music-hall idiom because he's not, in fact, interested in building up a detailed picture of what it's like to live in a council house in Barnsley. He is showing a social process at work: and so he takes characters that can be quickly read as accepted comic types, and then shows what happens to them when they are placed in unexpected situations.

So, at first, Mrs Jackson *talks* like a Coronation Street gossip. ('The rent collector give me your name . . . so I thought, well, I'd just pop round the door and have a word – like, it's your first day here, and why not be neighbourly, I thought . . .?') Arden draws on our stock responses. But as the story develops, these stock responses are undermined. At the end of the play, it is this conventional, ordinary, good-

neighbourly Mrs Jackson, who, affected by the presence of
the Sawneys, 'roars in her throat like a bull'. By using a
stock, good-neighbour figure, Arden is able to show, very
clearly, the potential violence in an apparently cosy neighbour-
hood.

The stock characters and music-hall gags belong to what
Arden calls the 'poetic' structure. Take, for example, the Old
Croaker's 'I tear them all up'. Tearing is one of the central
images of the play. 'How'd you like a real screaming sow to
raven your paunch for you, hey?' Rachel shouts to the
Official in the opening scene. 'What you want a lump of
raw meat shoved in the bars of the cage to tear at, *you* want,'
the respectable Jackson tells Rachel as he runs from her
bedroom. And the Old Croaker herself sings of her youth
'rooted out' and her pleasuring 'all torn down'.

In the hands of the Old Croaker, tearing becomes a
physical image. She goes through the play, like an ancient
female Harpo Marx, tearing up anything she can lay her
hands on, until she finally comes in with her arms full of
the neighbours' washing. The image of tearing is crystallized
as, faced by the neighbours baying in fury outside, the
Sawneys confront their own destruction by tearing the washing into shreds and throwing it over each other and all
round the stage. Arden has turned a music-hall gag into a
concrete image of the violence their presence has unleashed.
The anarchy of music-hall is linked directly with the anarchy
of a social situation. ('We're the old bones,' says Croaker to
Sailor at the end of the play. 'They tear us all up.')

Arden uses his music-hall idiom, therefore, to present a
clash of opposites. He shows us a situation in which conflict
is inevitable, and in doing so he implicitly asks us to question
the necessity for that situation. (This demonstrative aspect
of the play is emphasized by the use of the ballad which
warns us, Brecht-style, what each scene is going to be
about.)

But the music-hall idiom is linked as well with another aspect of the play – Arden's preoccupation with paradox and contradiction. The music-hall is essentially a theatre of paradox. A comedian is also a man who sings a sentimental song; backcloths are painted to represent real scenes, but remain obviously backcloths.

The final scene of *Live Like Pigs* is built around a series of contradictory images. There is a lullaby, and the sounds of a mob; a ragtime tune and broken windows; children's charms punctuated by the ringing of an ambulance bell; the killer Sailor lying helpless with a broken leg. The contradictory images are concrete expressions of the central paradox – that we are being shown outlaws rescued from the lawless violence of law-abiding citizens – by the police.

In a review of *Armstrong's Last Goodnight*, Edwin Morgan comments that *Live Like Pigs* has 'its undisclosed thesis – that people are, on the whole, neither reasonable nor flexible nor good-hearted, and that there is no real hope of bettering human society'.[1]

Morgan assumes that the play is making some comment on human nature, which he sees as an abstraction. Human nature is either reasonable and capable of betterment, he implies, or it's unreasonable – and Arden, he thinks, believes the latter.

But *Live Like Pigs* isn't talking about human nature. It's talking about a concrete situation. What the play does assert is that if you put people into an unreasonable situation then they are likely to behave unreasonably. In avoiding condemnation of either the Jacksons or the Sawneys, Arden is not taking up an amoral position. He is, on the contrary, showing a society whose way of treating people does violence to the way they want to live.

At the end of the play, both Sawneys and Jacksons have been destroyed by the contradictions. The Sawneys are

[1] *Encore*, July–August 1964, p. 48.

arrested, and old Sailor has 'fallen down'; the respectable
surface of the Jacksons' life has been torn to shreds with the
washing. But one of the characters refuses to be engulfed.
She's Rachel, who has referred to herself earlier as 'the real
screaming sow'. 'What does it matter which way,' she asks
at one point in the play, 'so you make your own true choice
of it?' Here, confronted with the authority of the police on
the one hand, and the demands for pity by the helpless
Sailor on the other, she makes her choice: 'they can chase
me to Northampton,' she says of the police: and, of Sailor,
'Heh! An old man with a broken leg.' And she picks up her
bundle and walks out of the insane situation.

   Live Like Pigs, then, shows us a situation in which conflict
and violence are inevitable, and it does so in the style of a
music-hall entertainment. But in 1958, it was easy to overlook
the stylization, to mistake the play for an exercise in social
realism that didn't come off. It was almost as if, in his first
play to be given a full-scale production, Arden felt the
necessity of coming closer to a style that was acceptable in
'legitimate' theatre terms. The play can, in fact, be produced
as a glum piece of illusion.

   But, as Pam Brighton demonstrated in a 1971 revival at
the Royal Court's Theatre Upstairs, it *needn't* be produced
that way. After fourteen years, the play remains one of the
funniest and most powerful statements about social conflict
in twentieth-century British theatre.

THREE: SERJEANT MUSGRAVE'S DANCE

(I)

Serjeant Musgrave's Dance is now generally accepted as John
Arden's masterpiece. It has been canonized by being made a
part of the English Literature 'A' level syllabus in schools:
and critics who disparage Arden's later work always refer

back to *Musgrave* as the peak of achievement against which everything else must be judged. But it wasn't always so. When the play was first produced, it was greeted with critical abuse. Now that the dust has settled, and the play's reputation is secure, it is possible to look more objectively at the causes of the original confusion.

They seem to me to centre on two uncertainties: an uncertainty of form, which Arden finally resolved in *Armstrong's Last Goodnight*; and an uncertainty relating to the presentation of the central character, Serjeant Musgrave himself.

In the matter of form Arden is feeling his way, in *Serjeant Musgrave's Dance*, from one kind of theatre to another. In *The Waters of Babylon* he had ignored completely the conventions of the theatre of illusion – and instead he had played with pantomime, direct speech, song, dance, slapstick. But in *Live Like Pigs* many of these devices had been discarded. Although the poetic structure was built round the music-hall, superficially the play could be squeezed inside the conventions of naturalist theatre. And, in the first two acts of *Serjeant Musgrave's Dance*, Arden creates a world which exists, out there on the stage, in its own right. It's only when, in the third act, he adopts the device of pretending that the audience in the theatre is also the crowd in the square of the mining town, that he re-establishes, through the Bargee, that direct recognition of the presence of the audience that is a part of the popular dramatic tradition – a recognition that was to become an essential feature in the style of all his plays after *Musgrave*.

Not that the first two acts have much in common with the naturalist conventions of the British theatre of the late 1950s. They are, in fact, closer to the movies, and, particularly, to those of the Hollywood western.

Stylistically, the script cries out for a camera. Again and again, in the middle of a scene, Arden cuts away from one

group of characters to another, as if he were picking people
out in close-up on a screen. In the opening scene, for example,
Sparky is standing guard on a canal wharf, while the two
other soldiers, Hurst and Attercliffe, are playing cards on
top of a drum. The scene opens with Sparky, cuts soon to
Hurst and Attercliffe ('The black spades carry the day . . .
We throw the red Queen over. . . .'), and then switches
back again to Sparky: 'How much longer we got to wait,
I'd like to know?' The sequence demands to be played in
terms of the shifting attention of a movie camera.

Again, the recruiting scene in Mrs Hitchcock's pub is
played in a sequence that alternates between shots of the
whole pub, and close-ups of the smaller groups. A song,
'Blow your morning bugles . . .' forms a background, but
between each verse, significant bits of action are picked out
in isolation. These slices of action are vital to the development of the story. In the theatre, one tends to be conscious
of the actors' determined efforts to keep the celebration
going, while not interfering with the important plot points:
in the cinema, the sequence would flow easily from group-
shot to close-up and back again.

It's not surprising that *Serjeant Musgrave's Dance* should
have a cinematic quality, since one of the central ideas of the
play sprang from an American film by Hugo Fregonese,
The Raid. Arden, in an *Encore* interview, describes the film
as follows. 'A group of men – Confederate soldiers in
disguise – ride into a Northern town. Three quarters of the
film is taken up with their installation in the town, and the
various personal relationships they establish. On the appointed morning, they all turn out in their Confederate
uniforms, hoist a flag in the square, rob a bank and burn
the houses. Finally . . . the cavalry arrives at the last minute,
although in this case they are too late.'[1]

In its structure, the play follows the film closely: but the

[1] *Encore*, July–August 1961, 'Building the Play', p. 26.

cinematic form of the first two acts creates its own problems for an audience.

For a western, however stylized, builds up its own world. That is to say, the story happens, out there, as a self-contained entity, not related to the audience in the cinema. And in the same way, Arden, in these two acts, creates a world that exists quite apart from the audience in the theatre. And although he uses the stage in a fluid way, and sprinkles the action with songs and verse, the fact that the world he creates *is* self-contained leads the audience towards a particular set of expectations. And among the expectations is included an ability to identify oneself with the man who appears to be the hero: Musgrave himself.

Arden is aware of the problem. 'Which character are you supposed to sympathize with in *Ghosts*?' he asks, and adds, 'It is merely that earlier plays in this manner have now become accepted. The trouble arises in the first performance of such plays, because the audience still looks for the character they are supposed to sympathize with. Once they know the play it is no longer necessary.'[1] But this is only another way of saying that Arden has not been able to build into the play a clear enough indication of 'the style of the entertainment' he is offering.

This is to some extent because Arden is borrowing from the language of one medium and applying it to another. If, as I've suggested already, Arden had been making a Hollywood movie with John Wayne as the star, he wouldn't have needed to teach the audience how to respond to Musgrave. But in the absence of an accepted convention, Arden tries to alienate Musgrave by the invention of an alter-ego in the shape of the Bargee.

Arden uses the Bargee throughout as a foil to Musgrave. Physically, the two are contrasted: Musgrave is 'the straightest serjeant on the line'; the Bargee is Crooked Joe. And

[1] *Ibid.*, p. 30.

Musgrave's actions are as rigid as his stance, while the Bargee's behaviour is as twisted as his body. Arden sets them against each other, in counterpoint on the stage.

There is, for example, the scene in which Musgrave delivers a prayer, 'God, my Lord God. Have You or have You not delivered this town into my hands?' Musgrave stands at the front of the stage, straight and upright, in his spotless scarlet uniform; while at the back of the stage, in grimy clothes, the Bargee parodies him. When, in imitation of Musgrave, the Bargee stands to attention, his body is comic and crooked, a question mark set against the straight backbone of the soldier. His mock reverence points up the absurdity of Musgrave's pose.

The relationship on stage between the two characters is very complex. Arden isn't using Musgrave to make the Bargee look cheap; and neither is he simply using the Bargee to cut Musgrave down to size. The two of them illuminate aspects of each other. So: Musgrave is tall, heroic. He is clearly to be admired. But (our eyes move to the Bargee) isn't there something a bit ridiculous about his stance? When you see the absurd pose of the Bargee, doesn't the soldier's pose look absurd, too? And yet, there's something noble about the soldier. Set against him, the Bargee looks like a cheap clown. And the soldier's message is so obviously right. . . . But isn't there something (the Bargee's actions suggest) also a bit exaggerated about Musgrave's language? What is all this about delivering the town into his hands? The Bargee's gestures make us aware of an element of self-dramatization in Musgrave's position. And yet, Musgrave's sense of purpose remains impressive.

Throughout the play, Arden builds up a dialectical relationship between Musgrave and the Bargee. The problem confronting any director of *Serjeant Musgrave's Dance* is how to preserve the dialectic. And, in fact, Arden himself only finds the real solution in the last act of the play, when he uses the Bargee as a direct intermediary between Musgrave and the audience. The Bargee comments to the audience on Musgrave's actions: and the relationship between the two of them becomes clear and precise. Musgrave is effectively distanced. We're able to watch his behaviour – and to judge it.

(2)

For all its uncertainties, *Serjeant Musgrave's Dance* remains, by any standards, a major achievement. To understand its strength, we need to turn from one source of Arden's inspiration – an American film – to another – the English ballad.

Arden writes:

> The bedrock of English poetry is the ballad. . . . Let me sketch a quick line of writers who have always built close to the bedrock. Chaucer, Skelton, Shakespeare, Jonson, Defoe, Gay, Burns, Dickens, Hardy, Joyce. All these men have known, almost as an unnoticed background to their lives, the enormous stock of traditional poetry, some of it oral, some of it printed and hawked at street-corners, some of it sung from the stages of music-halls. . . . They . . . form a line with strongly defined hereditary features, and they wrote from a basic unvarying poetic standpoint. . . . As seen through the eyes of the sort of writers I have mentioned, the English prove to be an extra-ordinarily passionate people, as violent as they are amorous, and quite astonishingly hostile to good government and order.[1]

If *Serieant Musgrave's Dance* is a western set in a north country town and brought to the stage, it is also a traditional ballad that deals, in Arden's words, 'with the concrete life of to-day'.[2]

In the ballads, Arden says, the themes are simple and general, and the colours primary:

[1] *Encore*, May–June 1960, 'Telling a True Tale', pp. 23–4.
[2] *Ibid.*, p. 22.

Black is for death, and for the coalmines. Red is for murder and
for the soldier's coat the collier puts on to escape from his
black. Blue is for the sky and for the sea that parts true love.
Green fields are speckled with bright flowers. The seasons are
clearly defined. White winter, green spring, golden summer, red
autumn.[1]

The story of *Serjeant Musgrave's Dance* has the simplicity of
a ballad. Four deserters bring the body of a dead soldier
back to his home town, a mining community in the grip of
a coal strike, and cut off by the winter snow. Their leader
plans to hold the town at gun-point, while, in a public
meeting, he presents the dead soldier's skeleton and brings
people face to face with the truth about war. But things go
wrong. One of the soldiers, Sparky, tries to run away with
a barmaid called Annie, and is accidentally killed. At the
climax of Musgrave's meeting, Annie produces Sparky's
body. The meeting collapses, the snow thaws, the dragoons
arrive, and one more of the deserters is killed. At the end
of the play the town celebrates its escape, while the two
remaining soldiers, Attercliffe and Musgrave himself, wait to
be hanged.

In an interview, Arden said:

> One of the things that set the play off was an incident in
> Cyprus. A soldier's wife was shot in the street by terrorists, and
> according to newspaper reports . . . some soldiers ran wild at
> night and people were killed in the rounding-up. The atrocity
> which sparks off Musgrave's revolt . . . is roughly similar.[2]

But, in *Live Like Pigs*, Arden had written a play he
describes as 'grey'. In putting together *Serjeant Musgrave's
Dance*, he wanted to begin with a primary colour, a scarlet
uniform. 'I used my historical imagination and decided that
the most likely character would be one of those Crimean

---

[1] *Encore*, May–June 1960, 'Telling a True Tale', p. 24.
[2] *Encore*, July–August 1961, 'Building the Play', p. 31.

Sergeants, who fought with rifle in one hand and Bible in the other.'[1]

The play is built around the primary colours. Musgrave is Black Jack, the straightest serjeant on the line. He reads a black Bible. In the opening scene, when Hurst and Attercliffe play cards, 'The black spades carry the day. Jack, King and Ace. *We* throw the red Queen over.'

The soldiers are red. 'Heheh . . . You know what they used to call 'em in them days – soldiers, I mean?' says the Bargee, at the beginning of the play. 'Blood-red roses, that was it. . . . Whack, whack, whack. Blood-red roses, eh? . . . That's right, now leave it where you've dropped it, and come ashore before you capsize her – you blood-red bloody roses, you!' The skeleton of Billy Hicks is white draped in red.

The miners, too, are black. Like death, 'A bayonet is a raven's beak.' In the celebration dance at the end ('Finnegan begin-agen,' whistles the Bargee, as he has whistled on his first appearance), they join hands with the red dragoons, who fill the stage, re-forming the circle of violence and counter-violence. But Musgrave and Attercliffe stand outside the circle.

At the centre of the play is a green apple. 'When I was a young lad,' says Attercliffe, 'I got married to a wife. And she slept with a greengrocer. . . . *I* saw him four foot ten inch tall and he looked like a rat grinning through a brush; but he sold good green apples and he fed the people and he fed my wife. I didn't do neither.'

In the final scene, as Musgrave and Attercliffe wait to be hanged, Arden pulls the play's imagery together in a song (sung by Attercliffe):

> I plucked a blood-red rose-flower down
> And gave it to my dear.

[1] *Ibid.*, p. 31.

I set my foot out across the sea
And she never wept a tear.

I came back home as gay as a bird
I sought her out and in:
I found her there in a little attic room
With a napkin round her chin.

Oh are you eating meat, I said,
Or are you eating fish?
I'm eating an apple was given me today,
The sweetest I could wish.

Your blood-red rose is withered and gone
And fallen on the floor:
And he who brought the apple down
Shall be my darling dear.

For the apple holds a seed will grow
In live and lengthy joy
To raise a flourishing tree of fruit
For ever and a day.

The imagery is clear. Musgrave has tried to end violence by
adding to the violence: 'Numbers and order. According to
Logic. I had worked it out for months.' 'To end it by its own
rules,' says Attercliffe. 'You can't cure the pox by further whoring.' The blood-red rose soldier has nothing to offer. Hope,
spring, is to be found in the green of the apple – the fruit
brought by the man who 'fed the people and . . . fed my wife'.
The last words of the play belong to Attercliffe, 'They're
going to hang us up a length higher nor most apple-trees
grow, Serjeant. D'you reckon we can start an orchard?'

(3)

'Complete pacifism,' writes Arden in the Introduction to *Serjeant
Musgrave's Dance*, 'is a very hard doctrine: and if the play
appears to advocate it with perhaps some timidity, it is prob-

ably because I am naturally a timid man – and also because I know that if I am hit I very easily hit back.'

Serjeant Musgrave's Dance is a play about a man who has an abstract idea about the way to end war. 'We are here with a word. That's all. That's particular. Let the word dance. That's all that's material.'

When he comes up against unexpected complexities, Musgrave can only insist that they are irrelevant. So, when he discovers that his skeleton, Billy Hicks, has been the father of Annie's dead child, he can only comment, 'It's not material. . . .' But he warns Mrs Hitchcock, 'What you've just been telling me, don't tell it to these. Dead men and dead children should bide where they're put and not be rose up to the thoughts of the living. It's bad for discipline.' (But he himself is planning to rise up the dead to the thoughts of the living.) And when Sparky is accidentally killed, trying to run away with Annie, Musgrave simply remarks, 'Desertion. Fornication. It's not material. He's dead. Hide him away.' Attercliffe knows better. When Annie produces the dead Sparky's coat, he cries, 'Oh, it's material. . . . I said it to you, Musgrave, it washes it all out.' And the radical miners' leader, Walsh – Musgrave's best hope in the town – adds, 'It bloody does and all, as far as I go.'

In his book, *The Liberal Imagination*, Lionel Trilling speaks of minds being 'violated by ideas'.[1] Musgrave has been raped by an idea. In pursuing this idea, he is incapable of taking into account the complexities he experiences. He drives rigidly forward, insisting that only logic matters, that accident isn't material. 'Our work isn't easy . . .' he tells Annie, 'It's got a strong name – duty. And it's drawn out straight and black for us, a clear plan. But if you come to us with what you call your life or love . . . and you scribble all over that plan you make it crooked, dirty, idle, untidy, *bad* – there's anarchy.' (The words

[1] Lionel Trilling, *The Liberal Imagination*, Secker & Warburg 1955, p. 288.

'crooked, dirty, idle' could apply, of course, to the Bargee – but his is a false anarchy that leads straight back to the dragoons and the re-formed circle.) 'The end of the world?' Musgrave says to Mrs Hitchcock. 'You'll tell me it's not material, but if you could come to it, in control; I mean, numbers and order, like so many ranks on this side, so many that, properly dressed, steadiness on parade, so that whether you knew you was right, or you knew you was wrong – you'd know it, and you'd stand. Get me summat to eat.'

Against Musgrave's 'Logic' Arden sets Mrs Hitchcock and Annie – and, in the end, Attercliffe. Annie answers Musgrave, not with logic, but with Sparky's torn coat. 'A bayonet is a raven's beak,' she says. 'This tunic's a collier's jacket. That scarecrow's a birdcage.' And Mrs Hitchcock tells Musgrave, 'Listen: last evening you told all about this anarchy and where it came from – like, scribble all over with life or love, and that makes anarchy. . . . Then *use* your Logic – if you can. Look at it this road: here we are, and we'd got life and love. Then *you* came in and you did your scribbling where nobody asked you. . . . There was hungry men, too – fighting for their food. But *you* brought in a different war.' 'God was with me,' replies Musgrave. 'God – and all they dancing . . .' But Mrs Hitchcock tells him, 'It's not a dance of joy. Those men are hungry, so they've no time for *you*. One day they'll be full, though, and the Dragoons'll be gone, and then they'll remember.'

Musgrave's mistake has been to isolate the 'Logic' from the true complexities of the situation. Compare Lionel Trilling's comment on liberalism, quoted on p. 29.

Serjeant Musgrave's Dance is a critique of the kind of liberal imagination that sees complexities as 'not material'; and of a crude pacifism that isn't aware that we live in a world in which, if we're hit, we very easily hit back.

But the critique is made, not in terms of a verbal argument, but in the image of a blood-red rose that falls – and a green apple that holds a seed. As Arden has said in another context: 'The action is the argument.'[1]

FOUR: THE HAPPY HAVEN

(1)

Although *Serjeant Musgrave's Dance* was at first given a generally hostile reception by the critics, it soon came to be accepted as an important play. It had all the necessary ingredients for importance: a serious theme, an equally serious central character, eloquent language and a tragic ending. Above all, the solemnity of the subject was matched by the dignity of the tone: *Musgrave* was a 'serious' play written in an equally 'serious' style.

This wasn't so obviously the case with Arden's next play, *The Happy Haven*, written (in collaboration with Margaretta D'Arcy) while he was a visiting Fellow in the Drama Department at Bristol University. *The Happy Haven*, which was first intended for an open stage, 'following roughly the Elizabethan model',[2] is a mixture of pantomime, music hall, high comedy and low farce. A ninety-year-old lady jumps out of her bath-chair to play hopscotch (and cheats into the bargain); hospital orderlies chase an imaginary dog round the stage; a doctor does a conjuring trick to turn liquid green, while an old man hides in his pyjamas under the lab bench; at the end of the play the doctor is turned into a baby boy. Moreover, the pantomime and the farce are centred on a theme that is generally accepted as being very solemn indeed: the social welfare of extremely old people. The Ardens treat this theme in an outrageously comic style. Most of the critics wrote off the play as a joke in bad taste.

The first and most important point to make about *The Happy Haven* is that it is a very funny play indeed – and demands to

[1] *Peace News* interview – see page 25 footnote (in *Encore* p. 16).

[2] Author's Note to *The Happy Haven* in *John Arden, Three Plays*, Penguin 1967, p. 193.

be presented as such. The farcical situations need to be played as farce, and not made half-heartedly 'realistic', because 'real' old people wouldn't behave like that. These aren't 'real' old people – if the play is produced as if they were, with actors tottering feebly about the stage, speaking their lines falteringly through trembling voices, then all the comic sharpness is lost, the pace drags and the fun evaporates. These characters are carefully stylized, formally presented, played by actors wearing masks. The play works best if the actors are young, athletic, physically boisterous, since the entertainment is hinged on the ludicrous contrast between old age and the way these characters behave on stage. The most obvious example of this is the scene in which Mrs Phineus defies the laws of possibility by playing hopscotch. The scene is funny *because* it's impossible: it comes as an outrageous physical surprise. But the impossibility makes us directly and physically aware of the reality of being old. The actors don't *become* old: but in being young they are able to *show* us old age. The more obviously young they remain, the more precisely they are able to pick out those aspects of old age they are presenting to us: and the funnier the show becomes.

But the fact that *The Happy Haven* is very funny doesn't prevent it from also being very serious. The Ardens are, in fact, asserting, through the form of *The Happy Haven*, that there are some subjects which are so serious and frightening that they can only be adequately dealt with in terms of farce. In *The Happy Haven*, they present us with a man who tries to conquer the deepest mysteries of nature and who ends as a baby, sucking a lollipop.

(2)

The Happy Haven is built round the figure of a scientist, Dr Copperthwaite, Superintendent of the Happy Haven, a 'hospital for the amelioration of the lot of the aged'. Copperthwaite at one point describes himself as 'a Doctor Faustus of the present generation', but he talks more like one of those popularizers of archaeology or astronomy on television programmes – a cross between a bureaucrat and a comic turn. Like Serjeant Musgrave, he has been raped by an idea: and like Musgrave, too, 'He's a professional man, dear,' as one of the patients says, 'he works to the rules'.

The Ardens demonstrate this professionalism in a number of comic scenes. In the opening scene, for example – in which they revert to the method of *The Waters of Babylon* and have Copperthwaite talking direct to the audience – Copperthwaite treats his patients with the remoteness of a salesman talking about cars. 'Aged seventy, all moving parts in good condition, cross-head pins perhaps slightly deteriorated, and occasional trouble from over-heated bearings when financial gain is in question.' If medical professionalism means not being emotionally involved with your patients, then Copperthwaite is a professional. Later, he speaks of them as being 'the raw material upon which I shall work'.

Elsewhere in the play, the Ardens show us Copperthwaite's professional bedside manner. He lays on a routine medical check for his patients, and keeps up an unchanging form of patter. 'Now there's no need to worry, Mrs Phineus, about all this bustling about and medical business. I just want a small routine check-up, nothing to it ... Say Ah. ... Ninety-nine. ... Waterworks all right? ... All right, me dear, off you go. ... X-rays ready, Robinson? ...Now for the next.'

As well as keeping up an engaging line in patter with the patients, Copperthwaite keeps one up with the audience.

'Excuse me, it's Sunday morning already, listen! (*The sound of church bells.*) I'm in a tearing hurry, the whole place is upside down, nothing prepared, and they'll be here in ten minutes. Who will? I can just spare sixty seconds to tell you.'

Talking to his rugger captain over the telephone, he shows the same kind of crude joviality, 'Watch it, Charlie, watch it,

c

she'll have you at the altar before you've buttoned your breeches. . . . All right Charlie, I'll remember. I'll put 'em in the post for you. Medical goods, a plain envelope. . . . We'll keep you a bachelor yet. . . . Yes, on the Health Service. Taxpayers for ever . . .'

But behind this jovial exterior, Copperthwaite is a man with an obsession. Like Musgrave, he has 'an over-riding purpose': and when he talks about this purpose, his 'professional detachment' crumbles away. 'But what I have here . . . ladies and gentlemen, is nothing less, or will be nothing less, than the Elixir of life – of Life, and of Youth. . . . If I am success-ful . . . then those five old people will not be at the end of their established term of years, but at the beginning! They will be able, they will be able, to be completely reborn! To any age we may see fit to lead them. Think of that. Think of that! . . . But let us preserve our professional detachment.'

Whenever Copperthwaite is involved with his research, his 'professional detachment' evaporates. When, for example, his routine experiments are interrupted by the arrival of one of the patients, the inquisitive Crape, his bedside manner is forgotten. 'You bloody dog, get out!' he cries. 'Oh, my God: coagulated.' Then he pulls himself together. 'I'm sorry, ladies and gentlemen. I'm afraid you're disappointed. We didn't reach it after all. But we will. Very shortly. It's a long road that has no turning.'

And when he actually discovers the Elixir, and the liquid turns green, he greets the discovery in rhapsodic terms, 'Beautiful. Oh my beautiful. Oh my lovely girl. Green as the leaves on the weeping willow tree, where my true love lies sleeping.' Then he adds, 'I've done it. I've done it. Gentle-men, you may smoke. One of mine?'

In the figure of Copperthwaite, the Ardens offer us a series of paradoxes. He is the apparently 'scientific' man, who, in moments of discovery, becomes a hack, romantic poet. He is the great genius, who is afraid of his rugger captain. He is the authority of an institution, who is bullied by his mother. And he is the man who has discovered the secret of life – and who tries it out on a dog in terms of, 'Come on, come on, doggie, good boy, good boy drinky, drinky, drinky.' In the end, literally, he becomes a little child. But the supreme irony is that his discovery is the result of accident. A patient arrives at the wrong moment: the stuff coagulates: and that is how the rational professionally-detached scientist unlocks the deepest secrets of nature.

(3)

To present Copperthwaite in this way, the Ardens have broken completely away from naturalist conventions. They use the stage partly as a music-hall platform and partly as a lecture theatre, in which Copperthwaite demonstrates scientific experiments which are also magic conjuring tricks. ('Accotile and heraclith solution? Good. You see what I'm doing? Watch for the change of colour . . .') The Ardens dispense altogether with illusion. To denote the passage of time, they simply have Copperthwaite walk from an upper stage to a lower stage and say, 'We can call it the next morning, now. . . .'

On to Dr Copperthwaite's lecture platform there erupt disturbing, unscientific elements in the shape of the five old people – 'Five green bottles hanging on the wall' who form the 'raw material' of his experiment. By using masks, stylization, formal speech, and the paradoxical device of having them shown by young actors, the Ardens are able to present these figures clearly and unsentimentally, with all their quirks and idiosyncracies and selfish obstinacies. There's no easy, *Cathy Come Home*-like appeal to our better nature. Look at them, say the Ardens: objectionable, impossible to live with, absurd, self-opinionated. That's what old people are like. Only remember, 'Your lives, too, will have their termination.'

The five old people are presented as 'humours' – that is to say, each of them has a particular characteristic which dominates his existence. To Mr Golightly, 'Love . . . is a star that will not turn. . . . *Love* is the meaning, say it is the conclusion.' (But when Mrs Phineus, to whom he professes his love, eats up the tomato sandwiches, he cries, 'Give her a bath. Hot, seething, pitch and brimstone. That's what she deserves.')

Mr Hardrader's life is built round his dog, Hector. He takes Hector for long walks and writes poems to him, which he delivers with all the élan of a music-hall entertainer:

> Old fellow. You and I through life
> Have wandered without hurt or strife
> Between us, man and dog.

The Ardens are able to make us laugh at Hardrader's absurdity, and yet still recognize Copperthwaite's monstrous behaviour in taking the dog away.

Mrs Letouzel's obsession is with Mrs Phineus's money. In a scene presented as a comic turn (it needs huge props, a giant pen and an enormous scroll of paper) she pretends to be taking care of Mrs Phineus's interests, while persuading her to sign away her investments. 'This narrow box more fruitful than the grave,' she sings as she cheats Mrs Phineus out of one more half-crown – 'for the Spastic Children Fund.'

Mrs Phineus is in her second childhood. She has always wanted a child, and when she plays a game and cheats, she cries, '*I* won, *I* won, *I* won. . . .'

Mr Crape, the final green bottle, holds the key to the play's development. He is the one who accidentally precipitates the experiment through nosing about in the doctor's lab. And he is nosing about because his obsession is with power.

In one of the central scenes of the play, he has the opportunity to demonstrate his power. The old people have discovered that they're all going to be rejuvenated. They're full of delight, gay and singing. But Crape, because he has a cold, has been declared negative. He confronts the old people, one by one, with their own illusions. If they did go back to their youth, he tells them, they would commit the same mistakes that would bring them back into Copperthwaite's power.

The climax of the play comes when the old people momentarily agree to act together against Copperthwaite. 'I am not a worm. My name is Henry Golightly and I walk upon legs,' says Golightly – but, ironically, his way of walking upon legs is to hide, pantomime style, under the lab bench while waiting to steal the Elixir. In a parody of a military exercise, the old people pin the distinguished visitors against the wall, and inject Copperthwaite with his own discovery. 'United we stand,' shouts Golightly, as Crape, who has instigated the action, tries to steal a drop of the Elixir to use on himself.

But behind the grotesque masks and the broad humours, the Ardens are able to confront us with the reality of old age. Playing the game of 'Truth or Die' with Crape, Mrs Phineus presents herself with stark objectivity:

> I'm an old old lady
> And I don't have long to live.
> I am only strong enough to take
> Not to give. No time left to give.
> I want to drink, I want to eat,
> I want my shoes taken off my feet.
> I want to talk but not to walk
> Because if I walk, I have to know
> Where it is I want to go. . . .
> Leave me be, but don't leave me alone.
> That's what I want. I'm a big round stone
> Sitting in the middle of a thunderstorm.
> There you are: that's true.
> That's me. Now: you.

The image of old age is a harsh one: and it's this image which the Ardens set against Copperthwaite's well-meaning but ultimately destructive bonhomie.

On one level, the play is a comic parable about the welfare state. The Happy Haven is a place where old people are fed and looked after – but where they're treated, not as people, but as raw material.

But on another level, the play questions a generally accepted attitude towards knowledge and experience. Copperthwaite isn't presented as a wicked man: but as a man whose imagination is limited, on one level, to rugby and rubber goods, but who is dabbling, on another level, with deep natural mysteries. And he dabbles with them in terms of, 'Put another nickel in. . . .'

The old people, for all their selfishness, obstinacy and absurdity, are involved with areas of experience Copperthwaite isn't even aware of. 'The life of man is lost and lonely,' sings Golightly near the beginning of the play – and the play shows the efforts of the old people to reach out of their loneliness. To Copperthwaite, such a concept doesn't exist.

In the end, *The Happy Haven* adds up to a statement about the destructiveness and frivolity and violence of a scientific attitude that sees human beings as objects in an experiment: but in making the statement the Ardens in no way evade the unpleasant qualities of the human beings themselves. 'Go home, and remember: your lives too will have their termination,' the old people tell the audience at the end. It's a harsh, uncompromising reminder – but it emerges from a play which is essentially gay, bouncy, and, above all, richly comic.

FIVE: THE WORKHOUSE DONKEY

> Some Critics said:
> This Arden baffles us and makes us mad:
> His play's uncouth, confused, lax, muddled, bad.
>
> Said Arden:
> Why do you accuse me and abuse me
> And your polite society refuse me,

Merely because I wear no belt nor braces?
There would be reason for the wry mouths in your faces
And reason for your uncommitted halting speeches
If you would but admit I wore no bloody breeches.

John Arden: Preface to *The Workhouse Donkey*

(1)

In *Serjeant Musgrave's Dance*, John Arden demonstrated the defeat of a man who tries to impose his own 'Logic' on 'anarchy'. In *The Happy Haven* he shows a group of grotesque individualists uniting to stage their own anarchic revolution against a man who claims to be rational, cool, detached. But in *The Workhouse Donkey*, which finally reached the stage in the summer of 1963, anarchy shifts from the edge to the centre of the play. *The Workhouse Donkey* is a celebration of anarchy: not the kind of anarchy that marches gloomily through streets, waving black banners and shouting slogans of love in tones of anger – but the anarchy of the Feast of Fools, with its Lord of Misrule, servants playing the roles of masters, naked girls riding on donkeys in York Minster, everybody, as Arden himself once put it, 'fucking everybody else in the streets'[1] and getting drunk. The play, in Arden's own words, gives

pride of place to the old essential attributes of Dionysus:

noise
disorder
drunkenness
lasciviousness
nudity
generosity
corruption
fertility
        and
ease.[2]

[1] *Peace News* interview.   [2] Preface to *The Workhouse Donkey*.

That it was first staged and then buried in the staid environment of Chichester, in the summer of the Profumo scandal and the arrival of the Beatles, says a great deal about the *rigor mortis* of those who controlled – and, for the most part, still control – the British theatre. 'There is a sort of solemnity about people in the theatre,' Arden said, in a *Peace News* interview just after the first production. 'You get somebody like Lord Chandos on the National Theatre board and the mind boggles. I wouldn't like to think that the theatre in the next few years was going to be run between the Aldwych and the National rather like the world is run between Moscow and Washington. . . .'[1] Already, in 1963, there were signs of the conflicts that would later erupt at the time of *The Hero Rises Up*, and that have, at the time of writing (1972), apparently driven the Ardens out of the theatre.

The basic story of *The Workhouse Donkey* is simple. A man of excessive integrity, Feng, is appointed Chief of Police in a northern town run by a Labour caucus, headed by a man of equally excessive corruption, Charlie Butterthwaite – the Napoleon of *The Waters of Babylon*. Because of their extremes of temperament and belief, the two clash. The town is torn apart, and they are both destroyed in the process, leaving the more moderately corrupt middle-of-the-roaders to form a coalition in praise of whitewash at the end.

But if the story is simple, the plot is extremely intricate. It twists and turns in every scene, offering mind-boggling surprises: and it's developed with a richness of texture that even Arden has previously never equalled. It's this richness that makes the play such an anarchic and liberating experience.

Take, for example, one of the central scenes – the visits of Butterthwaite and his fellow Labour Councillors to the Copacabana Club, in search of evidence that the police, in collusion with the local Tories, are conniving at obscenity. The scene has three purposes: to develop the plot, to offer a social

[1] *Peace News* interview (reprinted in *Encore* September–October 1965).

comment about the ultimate dreariness of the strip club world – but also to create in the audience a sense of release and enjoyment, to 'inflame people's lusts'.

The scene is put together with the precision of a Whitehall farce. Butterthwaite is visiting the club in search of proof of police corruption; only he happens to have accidentally chosen the night of a police raid, and we wait for him to get caught; only the police have tipped off the club, and Butterthwaite also hears about this. And so, when the police arrive, we watch them solemnly going through the ritual, in plain clothes, of asking for drink and being given coffee, and equally solemnly telling Superintendent Wiper (who's having an affair with the manageress, Gloria) that, 'Upon our arrival here, sir, dancing was in progress in a normal fashion' and that the licensing laws 'were being properly observed' – only for Butterthwaite suddenly to turn round at the end and say, 'As a magistrate and a leading citizen, *I* desire to lay an information against the conduct of this club.' The twist is completely unexpected: and Butterthwaite adds to its arrogance by advising the girls he's just informed on to join a trade union.

Within this farcical framework – itself a delight – Arden is able to make a number of sharp, and funny, social observations. These spring mainly from the incongruity of the Labour Councillors in a would-be sophisticated environment – Arden uses these opposites to comment satirically on each other. 'We don't serve Guinness, I'm afraid, sir. . . . Certainly whisky. . . . But I'm afraid there's no drinks allowed without something to eat.' 'We had us suppers already,' says Hardnutt: and when the waitress says all they need to order is a sandwich, Hickleton asks, 'We don't have to have a sandwich every time we refill, do we?' Later Butterthwaite comments, 'And they call this a sandwich! It's not even got a top on.' When Butterthwaite tries to order 'a Babycham for t'young lady', the Hostess says, 'It's all right. She's brought it. . . . just the telegraph.' 'Damned expensive telegraph . . . fifteen-and-six for one Babycham. . . .'

Arden is mocking the Labour Councillors' lack of sophistication – we laugh, to some extent, at their lack of experience. But he's also mocking the sophistication itself, the pretensions of the place, with its open sandwiches and its fifteen-and-six Babychams. Young Sweetman, the son of the Tory leader, totters across the room towards Butterthwaite. 'I represent the standards of civilization in this paleo-paleo-paleolithicalolithealithic community. I've had an education,' and he falls into a Hostess's lap.

The girls themselves are victims of this pseudo-sophistication. At one point they appear wearing bells and balloons. 'The difficulty was,' writes Arden, 'to get the girls . . . to look first of all attractive and provocative to the audience, then attractive and provocative to the other characters on the stage, and then to look as if they were girls who were just doing this for a living, and a rather dreary kind of living when it's all added up.'[1] In the Chichester production, they sang an absurd song:

> Poppety, pop, pop a balloon . . .
> ring a ding, ding, ring a little bell.

(It was, perhaps, the only happy invention of the production – but it lost most of its points, since 'I wanted them to be dressed in nothing but bells and balloons . . . but . . . the management had to send to the Lord Chamberlain a description of what other garments they were wearing, which obviously had to be adequate, with the result that they looked far too adequate, by no means warranting the attention of the police, which is what the plot implied.'[2] The girls were to look sexy – but were also to remind the audience that commercialized sex is ultimately, 'just dead and unfulfilled'. In other words, they were to be funny and absurd, and one's

[1] *Peace News* interview (see page 25 footnote).   [2] *Ibid.*

mind was to register the absurdity: but they were also to be enjoyable, pretty girls taking their clothes off.

In the Chichester production, the absurdity was achieved, but not the lust – simply because the girls were not allowed, by the Lord Chamberlain, to be erotic enough.

Much of the scene's sense of anarchy is, however, carried, not by the girls, but by Butterthwaite himself. If both the Labour Councillors and the sophistication of the club are cut down to size, Butterthwaite remains, throughout, a huge, out-size figure. When the Councillors arrive at the club, he first has Hardnutt bribe the doorman out of Labour Party funds, and then says, 'See what I mean? They're breaking the law already. Note the time.' Once inside, he determines to make the most of the evening. 'Now then, Charlie, watch it,' says Hopefast. 'We're disinterested observers.' 'Disinterested bloody slag-ladles,' cries Butterthwaite. 'We're full members of this joint, and we're going to take advantage.' 'Use a bit of aesthetic appreciation,' he tells Hardnutt, who is complaining about the price of a Babycham. 'I'm here to enjoy myself. . . . Go on, tear it off, I want to see the lot.' With undisguised lechery, he makes the most of what's going; ridicules the police when they arrive ('He's an agent provocative, but so long as it's clearly understood all round no harm need be done'), and then, with sublime effrontery, lays evidence against what he has just been enjoying. 'We have just witnessed a demonstration of the passing about among the tables of four little doxies dressed in nowt but balloons – or, in the case of two of them, bells – which we were invited to burst or to tingle as the case may be.' And, having informed on the girls, he tells them, 'I didn't come here to deprive you of your livelihoods. However, in the fell and calamitous grinding of two mighty opposites, someone has to go to t'wall. And them wi' fewest clothes on o' force gets squeezed hardest! Do all o'you girls belong to a union?' Butterthwaite creates around himself the anarchy of the Feast of Fools.

This richness of texture is there throughout the play. As in *The Waters of Babylon*, characters break out suddenly into song and dance – or else reveal themselves and their dreams in formal verse. So, the prosaic Young Sweetman, who is not shown to be very bright, and whose conversation is halting and full of clichés, is suddenly inspired to poetry by his love for Wellesley:

> As I was lying on my bed
> And my eyelids blue with sleep
> I thought I saw my true love enter,
> Golden and dusty were her feet.
> Her gown of green, it let be seen
> Her shoulders white and brown,
> Her hair was tied in a high tight ribbon
> As sleek as a pool of trout
> And her earlobes like the Connemara Marble
> Moved quietly up and about.

'As I breathed, I suppose?' says Wellesley – and Young Sweetman brings the scene back to earth by saying, 'As you breathed, and as you were eating.'

Sir Harold Sweetman, Tory leader, and head of a brewery and cornflakes factory, reveals himself as a Shakespearian hero in disguise. (In a theatre workshop exercise, we gave him a cardboard crown and a toy sword: he hid them to make a fat belly under his pyjamas – and brought them out when his wife had gone to bed.) He declaims to the audience, like a budding Richard III:

> It has been argued and by no less a voice
> Than that of the Prime Minister, that today
> Class-struggle is concluded. All can rise
> Or fall according to desire or merits
> Or (it may be) according to finance.
> I am as rich as any man in Yorkshire,
> I brew good beer and drink my own good product.
> I fabricate perfected breakfast food

And crunch it with my family round my table.
Both beer and breakfast food are drunk and crunched
By simultaneous millions through the land.
So Sweetman should have risen, so he has.
But to what eminence? . . .
I am a prince, I am a baron, sirs!
And yet, I have no sovereignty, no. . . .
The election lights on Butterthwaite – not once
But three times three, or nine times nine, I fear.

The incongruity between the heroic style of the verse and its content – local politics, a brewery, cornflakes – opens up a whole, frustrated realm of the Tory Councillor's imagination.

Boocock, the Labour leader, has a similar moment of truth. For most of the play, we're able to take up a comfortable, superior attitude to Boocock. He's the honest, not over-bright local politician who never fully understands what is going on. When Butterthwaite complains that Feng is hobnobbing with the Tories at a dinner party, and adds, 'Why couldn't you have invited him to dinner yersen?' Boocock replies, 'He's welcome any time to tek a sup o' tea wi' me and Mrs Boocock.' 'Oh, Barney, Barney, Barney,' says Butterthwaite, 'you've no bloody notion, have you?'

In a poem, Arden demonstrates the limitations of Boocock's political imagination:

We're up here to show the Tories
How honest men can rule.
We've built a playground for the little children
And a comprehensive school.
We lead the whole West Riding
In our public schemes of housing,
And for the drainage of the town,
In pre-stressed concrete firm and strong
That not an H-bomb can ding down,
The Borough Engineer's contrived
A revolutionary outfall. . . .

Boocock's imagination, in the age of possible nuclear destruction, is limited to the building of a 'splendid new Town Hall'; to him, the Labour politician, revolution is a new drainage scheme.

But, suddenly, Arden shifts the tone, and Boocock begins to talk in a much more personal way:

> It comes a rugged reflection
> To a rude old man like me
> Who's had no ease to his efforts
> Nor helpful education:
> That in the hour of his honour
> And the heaping of red robes
> And gold chains of his glory
> He sets up a strong staircase
> For to stride up in his pride:
> And reaches nowt but rheumatics
> Nosing theirselves northward
> From his knee to his ribcage!

Boocock has been good for an easy laugh: suddenly, Arden forces on us an entirely different awareness of his character: and he does so by breaking the narrative surface and allowing Boocock to present himself directly in a simple statement.

'I never write a scene so that the audience can identify with any particular character,' Arden says. 'I try and write the scene truthfully from the point of view of each individual character.'[1] And so, in presenting Feng, the authoritarian Chief Constable, Arden is not concerned with taking up an easy satirical position, but with trying to show what makes him tick.

Feng's opening speech is a collection of clichés. 'We live in an age of overthrown moral standards. The criminal today is coddled and cosseted by the fantastic jargon of mountebank psychiatry. . . .' We think we know where we are with him,

---

[1] *Peace News* interview – see page 25 footnote (in *Encore* p. 15).

particularly when he begins to repeat the speech to Wellesley at the Tory cocktail party. 'What about the moral standards of the British policeman?' she asks. 'Are his overthrown as well?'

But gradually Arden forces on to us a respect for Feng. When Sweetman and his crony advise him to raid Butterthwaite's pub, he says:

> I should be glad of relevant information,
> Or none at all. I do not know you, sir,
> I do not know this people. And I must test
> The whole community according to
> The rigid statutes and the statutes only.
> I can assure you now without vainglory
> My testing will be thorough.

'Are you quite sure he's ours?' Young Sweetman asks his father: and when, later, one of the Tories asks him whose side he's on Feng replies, 'Side . . . side! I am not, sir, aware of it.'

Feng seems to be the completely independent man of integrity, but in his scenes with the girl, Wellesley (illegitimate daughter of Butterthwaite's 'fixer', the corrupt Dr Blomax), he reveals an unexpected vulnerability. 'I am, alone, not sufficient,' he tells her, 'in fact I am bewildered. Particularly now, surrounded as I am by a confusion of democracy and alien loyalties, for support I turn – where? Of necessity to another alien. I would like you to become my wife.'

The proposal is as surprising as it is formal: but it is also logical. Arden confronts us with a paradox. To preserve his integrity, Feng must stand alone, outside a corrupt society. But if he stands outside, he is no longer able to understand and control that society. And so he turns to 'another alien' for help: with the result that he is, irretrievably, entangled in the corruption. When Wellesley's father, Blomax, turns Queen's evidence on Butterthwaite, Feng says, 'It is unusable, I'm afraid.' The reason why it's unusable is that someone who gives Queen's evidence can't be prosecuted: and Feng won't

allow anybody to think that, simply because he's in love with
Wellesley, he's allowing her father to go free. 'Have you ever
seen a boa-constrictor that strangled itself with itself?' cries
Wellesley: and Sweetman adds, 'But in fact you're telling me
that if it wasn't for this little half-dago doxy that bloody
robber Butterthwaite would have been behind bars a week
since!'

Feng's integrity in the end defeats itself. But his fall is not
that of a ludicrous comic figure, but of a tragic hero in a non-
heroic society (which means, of course, that he is still somewhat ridiculous):

> Not long ago
> In this elected Council there was in violence
> Raised a violent demand I should resign.
> I did not notice it. I said that I
> Derived authority for my high office not
> From the jerk and whirl of irrelevant faction –
> You, sir, and you, your democratic Punch and Judy –
> But from the Law, being abstract, extant, placed,
> Proclaimed 'I am'! But, as you say, sir, now,
> Violence and damage, I *do* resign, sir, now . . .
> Continue, Mr Wiper . . . Preserve the peace.

Arden says:

I feel he is a good man, who behaves in a way dictated by
feelings of the utmost integrity, and concludes by doing a
tremendous amount of damage. Whereas on the other hand
Butterthwaite is a pretty scoundrelly sort of person. . . . But my
view is that the type of corruption he represents does a great
deal less harm to a community of people where it is understood
and lived with than the type of ferocious integrity implied in
the figure of the Chief Constable. Now this is not a view I
would expect everybody to share. . . . But if you dramatize a
conflict and you say, one side in my opinion is white, the other
side is black, and you underrate the strength, integrity and
commonsense of the black side, then you will give your side an

easy walkover. Well, you wouldn't be writing the play if your side had an easy walkover. It wouldn't be necessary to make this propaganda if there wasn't a serious struggle involved – therefore why not be fair?[1]

Arden presents Feng with careful fairness.

But, without doubt, the richest figure in the play is Butterthwaite himself. At the beginning of the play, Butterthwaite is presented as part-clown, part-charlatan, and part-idealist. He has the music-hall comedian's patter, 'Any young lass down there want the icing smoothed over her wedding-cake?'; the demagogue's matiness, 'What's your consistency? I like to see good workmanship'; and the typical Labour politician's trick of making a sentimental appeal to history:

> And as far as this town goes, *we're* t'masters now. It warn't so easy to credit that in 1897 when your old uncle Charlie first saw the light of day in the lying-in ward of the Municipal Workhouse. And 1926 I call to my memory as a year of some bitterness, too. I fancy Sir Harold Sweetman bears those days in mind. He and his confederates. They beat us at the time. But we fought and fought again, and in the end we won. And that's the end o' that.

Though a Labourite, Charlie has none of Boocock's puritanism. 'Ah, we don't want to interfere with the pleasures of our gilded youth, Barney,' he says, when Boocock complains about the Copacabana Club. And he is corrupt on a majestic scale. He can rail in righteous indignation against Feng dining with the Tories, and in the same breath berate Boocock for not having invited Feng to dinner himself. His way of dealing with a Tory proposal to turn the Municipal Hospital Annexe back into an art gallery is to form an emergency committee meeting of the Ways and Means Committee in the saloon bar of the Victoria and Albert after hours and vote it out, without even telling his own party leader. Corruption to

---

[1] *Peace News* interview – see page 25 footnote (in *Encore* pp. 15–16).

Butterthwaite has become a throwaway line, 'Every single meeting of the Hospital Management Committee has confirmed the state of affairs. Dammit, the Chairman is my cousin's brother-in-law. I ought to know.'

His corruption is allied to an intense appetite for enjoyment. Behind the blarney, this, to Butterthwaite, is what politics is all about. At the Copacabana, he'll spend Labour Party funds, feel up the girls and give information against them without any sense of contradiction. And when he talks about his reign, it's not in terms of comprehensive schools, revolutionary drainage schemes and new town halls. 'Oh, oh, oh, I have lived. I have controlled,' he says. 'I have redistributed. . . .The tables have been spread. Not with bread and marge, . . . but with a summation of largesse demanding for its attendance soupspoons in their rack, fish-knives and forks, flesh-knives and forks, spoons for the pudding, gravy and cruet, caper sauce and mayonnaise . . . and I by my virtue stood the President of the Feast!'

Butterthwaite is, in every way, outsize – in his corruption, his generosity, his appetite, and above all, in his arrogance. But it's not mainly his arrogance that in the end leads to his downfall. It's a peculiar kind of innocence – similar to the innocence Johnnie Armstrong shows, in *Armstrong's Last Goodnight*, when he dresses up, like a child, in his gay clothes, and, believing in Lindsay's promise of a safe-conduct, goes unarmed to his death.

Butterthwaite has a friend in Doctor Blomax. As Blomax says, 'every emperor needs to have his dark occult councillor: if you like, his fixer, his manipulator – me. I do it because I enjoy it.' Blomax, too, is corrupt: but there is none of Butterthwaite's innocence in his corruption. He is always the cunning calculator, exerting a little pressure here, a little blackmail there, and bowing to events when he needs to. Butterthwaite owes him money, for gambling debts; and the town cabal, in its determination to ruin Butterthwaite, bribes and blackmails Blomax into asking for the money. 'Over-indulgent prescriptions,' he tells Butterthwaite. 'I only regarded it as an extension of a normal bedside manner. But it looks like coming up at a coroner's inquest, so I've got to pay up or hic, haec, hoc, I'm done.' 'Are you telling me the truth?' asks Butterthwaite; and when Blomax replies, 'The absolute and clear-starched verity,' it never occurs to Butterthwaite to doubt his friend. It's this naive trust in Blomax – and also in his own power – that leads Butterthwaite to over-reach himself. Earlier in the play he has asked Blomax, 'And what'd you expect me to do for you if you were [being pressed for t'cash]? Burgle t'town hall?' And now, at the height of his power, with Feng apparently at his mercy, this is precisely what he does. And he does it with that carefree assurance that characterizes all his actions. As he opens the safe and takes the money out, he comments, 'There's nigh on a thousand in here. I don't know how many times I've had to tell these skiving clerks this is *not* the Barclays Bank! . . . Ho, there's some head going to roll in this office tomorrow morning.'

It's in this scene of the burglary that Arden crystallizes the image of the donkey – 'an image expressing lust and anti-social behaviour and bad smells, generally rather a disgusting little animal'. Before Butterthwaite scatters the money, 'indicating a similitude of ludicrous panic', he sings a song – Arden completely breaks the naturalist surface to present 'the poetic issue':

> In the workhouse I was born
> On one Christmas day
> Two long ears and four short feet
> And all I ate was hay.
>
> Hay for breakfast, hay for dinner,
> Lovely hay for tea,
> I thanked my benefactors thus:
> Hee-haw hee-haw *hee*!

The 'benefactors' thrust the donkey out into the world ('You've grown up quite disgusting'), and once again the donkey thanks them:

> I could not understand, you see,
> Just how it was they thought of me
> Or what it was they saw!

'What it was they saw' becomes clear in the next verse:

> The street was full of folk, they said,
> He's got two ears upon his head
> He's got four feet upon his legs
> He's got . . . My God, look what he's got,
> They cried, Get back to France!
>
> I said – hee-haw – you're very rude
> I do the best I can.
> You couldn't treat me worse, I said,
> If I was a human man!

'And the minute I said that they all fled away'. Left alone in the street, the donkey sees himself in a mirror in a pawn-broker's shop:

> O what a shock, I nearly died,
> I saw my ears as small as these,
> Two feet, two hands, a pair of knees,
> My eyeballs jumped from side to side,
> I jumped right round, I bawled out loud,
> You lousy liars, I've found you out!
> I know now why you're fleeing . . .
> I am no donkey, never was,
> I'm a naked human being!

In the song, Arden is summing up the theme of the play. Butterthwaite is a threat to the people in the town who want to keep their corruptions hidden and respectable. His outsize, anarchic corruption, even more than Feng's integrity, is a threat to their way of life. And so they put him out and heap their sins upon him. He becomes the scapegoat.

Butterthwaite's threat to the town's polite corruption is made concrete in his two visits to the Copacabana Club. The club is an image of the town's respectable obscenities. It's financed by the Tory leader, patronized by his son, and managed by the mistress of the police superintendent – the affair between Wiper and Gloria is a clear image of the town's toleration of a limited corruption. And the girls in the club offer naughtiness, not orgy: 'Poppety pop, pop a balloon.'

The visit of the donkey ('My God, look what he's got') destroys both the acceptable naughtiness and the social collusion. 'Go on, tear it off,' he shouts to the girls, 'I want to see the lot!' He threatens to bring orgy into the niceness – 'Control yourself, Alderman,' says the high priestess of this suburban temple of mild vice. More important, he threatens the hypocritical social relationships. He exposes the collusion between the guardians of law and the practitioners of sin.

The transformation of the Copacabana Club into an art gallery is an image of the town's response, both to Feng and to Butterthwaite's actions. The dirt is carefully swept under the carpet. Blomax makes the point explicit, 'Who indeed would recognize the premises themselves, where the only indication of what's under the underwear is on a canvas by Titian . . . or at least William Etty?' The donkey's great crime has been to expose openly 'what's under the underwear', and for this he is to be put out.

The image is made concrete in the scene of Butterthwaite's second visit – this time to the opening of the art gallery, on May Day. He invades the ceremony at the head of a crowd of drunks and layabouts, the 'lousy' of the town. 'Well, Charlie's lousy too,' he tells them, 'and Charlie bears in mind that the first day of May is not only a day of Socialist congratulation but also a day of traditional debauchment in the base of a blossoming hedgerow.' Sitting on the table, with the crockery swept to the floor, draped in a tablecloth and wearing a garland of flowers, he finally becomes the Lord of Misrule.

And his Lord of Misrule is also a parody of the Jesus who rode triumphantly on a donkey on Palm Sunday:

> In my rejection I have spoken to this people. I will rejoice despite them. I will divide Dewsbury and mete out the valley of Bradford; Pudsey is mine, Huddersfield is mine, Rotherham also is the strength of my head, Ossett is my lawgiver, Black Barnsley is my washpot, over Wakefield will I cast out my shoe, over Halifax will I triumph. Who will bring me into the strong city, who will lead me into the boundaries of Leeds? Wilt not thou, oh my deceitful people, who has cast me off? And wilt not thou go forth with Charlie?

The speech is a hilarious Feast of Fools parody of Jesus, lamenting over Jerusalem – Jerusalem is ludicrously replaced by Ossett, Dewsbury and the other Yorkshire towns, and the Messiah is a drunken rogue. When one of Butterthwaite's disciples, carried away by the rhetoric, cries, 'We're all going forth together,' Butterthwaite deflates the rhetoric with, 'The only place you're going is into t'black maria.'

At the end of the scene, Charlie (donkey/scapegoat/comic Jesus) is literally carried out. As he goes, he sings again. In the Chichester production, the song was turned into a dirge, mournful, slow. But what Arden had in mind was the gay, jaunty signature tune of Z-Cars:

> Out he goes the poor old donkey
> Out he goes in rain and snow,
> For to make the house place whiter
> Who will be the next to go?

The song isn't a lament: there's nothing self-pitying about Charlie Butterthwaite. Always he sees himself and his own position with humour; and his parting words are gay and defiant:

> When all is washed and all is scoured
> And all is garnished bright as paint,
> Who will come with his six companions
> And a stink to make you faint?

The reference is, of course, to the New Testament parable of the man who drove out one devil only to have seven others take the first one's place. Butterthwaite is asserting in the song that what he represents can't be disposed of by a 'commendably accomplished' police action.

But the people who are left after Feng and Butterthwaite are gone assert the opposite:

> We smell as we think decent.

They unite to tell the alien theatre audience:

> If we tell you we've cleaned our armpits
> You'd best believe we've cleaned 'em recent.
> We have washed them white and whiter
> Than the whitewash on the wall
> And if for THE WORKHOUSE DONKEY
> We should let one tear down fall
> Don't think by that he's coming back . . .
> The old sod's gone for good and all!

As usual, Arden doesn't try to resolve the contradiction. He simply presents it, and leaves it at that.

(2)

The Workhouse Donkey works on a number of different levels: as an intricate and entertaining story, as the dramatization of a clash between 'two mighty opposites', as a comment on local politics, as an anarchic celebration. But, at the simplest level, the play is as packed with entertainment as a popular variety show. There are boisterous songs:

> I married my wife because I had to,
> Diddle di doo: Di doo doo – doo . . .

and an endless stream of gags. A medical examination ends in a dance; a committee meeting is played like a game of musical chairs; a detective spies on a man by reading a newspaper with a hole cut in the middle; a night watchman, finding the money from the town hall safe strewn about the floor, does a classic double-take – 'I never knew a more careless lot in all my born days. The place could have been robbed ten times over.' Each scene demands to be played as a turn in its own right, with the emphasis, not on 'character' and 'motivation', but on putting over the songs and the jokes.

The one level the play can't work on is that of straight naturalism. Naturalism demands the creation of psychologically convincing characters, and imposes its own concept of the plausible. Geoffrey Reeves, talking about a production he directed in Denmark, describes how the actor who played Charlie 'simply couldn't conceive why Charlie would rob the safe';[1] and Ronald Hayman, in his book on Arden, comments: 'The most implausible moment of all comes when Butterthwaite burgles the safe.'[2]

But the whole point of *The Workhouse Donkey* is that human behaviour *can* be richly and grotesquely and joyfully implausible. Arden once said:

> When I was working on *The Workhouse Donkey* I began to feel psychologically more and more disorientated . . . and that having conceived the idea of this respected and powerful borough councillor, who is at the height of his power, and who then suddenly, for no apparent reason . . . just tosses it all in the air and says, 'Fuck you, I'm through' – well, I began to feel in some peculiar way I ought to do the same thing. And this is one of the reasons for possibly the looseness of construction of parts of the play, which seems to have annoyed the critics. I began quite gratuitously to put in scenes for no very good reason other than that I thought they might upset Philip Hope-Wallace.[3]

[1] *Encore*, September–October 1965, 'Arden, Professionals and Amateurs', p. 30.
[2] *John Arden*, Heinemann Educational Books, London, 1968, p. 48.
[3] *Peace News* interview – see page 25 footnote (in *Encore* p. 17).

The form of *The Workhouse Donkey* embodies Arden's rejection of a narrow, limited concept of 'legitimate' theatre; the content of the play equally embodies his rejection of a limited concept of 'plausible' behaviour.

The Workhouse Donkey, in the end, affirms that the outrageous and the implausible are only to be expected. But the affirmation demands an equally bold and outrageous form of theatre. So far the play, quite simply, hasn't had the production it deserves.

SIX: ARMSTRONG'S LAST GOODNIGHT

Armstrong's Last Goodnight was the last of Arden's major plays to reach London. It was produced at Chichester in the summer of 1965, a few weeks after the opening of *Left-Handed Liberty* at the Mermaid. But *Armstrong's Last Goodnight* was written before *Left-Handed Liberty*, and had been presented, in a slightly different form, by the Glasgow Citizens' Theatre in 1964.

Armstrong's Last Goodnight is, in many ways, a sequel to *Serjeant Musgrave's Dance*. Like *Musgrave*, it deals with an attempt to stop violence; like *Musgrave*, it springs from an historical situation – this time, the war in the Congo that followed the proclamation of independence (the play is dedicated to Conor Cruise O'Brien, who was responsible for United Nations action in the Congo after the murder of Lumumba); and, like *Musgrave*, it is linked with the ballad in form – and also, as William Gaskill, who directed the National Theatre production, points out, with the western. But, whereas *Serjeant Musgrave's Dance* has as its chief protagonist a gloomy, fanatical, Bible-thumping figure, *Armstrong's Last Goodnight* is built round a literate, civilized diplomat. Musgrave had tried to cure the pox by further whoring: Lindsay, in *Armstrong's Last Goodnight*, believes that if you treat the pox playfully enough it will go away.

The play is set in sixteenth-century Scotland. A precarious peace is being negotiated between Scotland and England, but it's constantly threatened by the activities of the border outlaws. Lindsay, the herald and tutor of the young Scottish king, sets himself the task of bringing the most notorious of these outlaws, Johnny Armstrong of Gilnockie, 'Intil the King's peace and order'. In the process, he brings together against himself powerful enemies at court, and he almost compromises himself with the English. But it is only when his own highland secretary, McGlass, is stabbed, almost inconsequentially, by a fanatical Evangelist with whom Gilnockie has associated himself, that Lindsay finally accepts 'the gravity of ane other man's violence'. He offers Gilnockie a safe-conduct, and then has him captured and hanged.

This bloody and barbarous story is presented to the audience by Lindsay in the urbane tones of a sixteenth-century court poet. Formalistically, Lindsay takes over where the Bargee in *Musgrave* leaves off. In the last act of *Musgrave*, the Bargee stands between the audience and the action: throughout *Armstrong*, Lindsay acts as a direct mouthpiece to the audience, offering the events and himself for their consideration. From the very first speech, he establishes an attitude that is both gay and sardonic:

> There was held, at Berwick-upon-Tweed, in the fifteenth year of the reign of James the Fift . . . and in the nineteenth year of Henry the Eight . . . ane grave conference and consultation betwixt Lords Commissioner frae baith the realms, anent the lang peril of warfare that trublit they twa sovereigns. . . . As ye will observe: when peace is under consideration, there is but little equability of discourse.

Throughout the opening scene of discussion and manœuvring between the English and the Scots Commissioners, Lindsay stands on the roof of the Palace, a silent observer. The result is that we watch the diplomatic moves through his sceptical and amused eyes.

Not only is the tone that of a courtly poet. The language, too, is a sharp and accurate pastiche of Lindsay's own play, *The Three Estates*. In dealing with this subject Arden was confronted with a particular problem of language. He partly took as a model Arthur Miller's *The Crucible*, in which Miller invented a formalized version of early American speech. Arden has invented a similarly formalized version of the dialects of the Scottish Lowlands: but whereas Miller's invention led merely to a somewhat windy rhetoric, Arden's has the wit and economy of the best verse of the period:

> The rags and robes that we do wear
> Express the function of our life.
> But the bawdy body that we bear
> Beneath them carries nocht
> But shame and greed and strife.
> It is pleisand to naebody
> Of its hairy sweat and nudity;
> Save belike to ane cruel tormentor
> Whaur his whip will leave the better bloody mark,
> Or save belike to our ain rejoict Creator,
> Whaur he walks through the green glade
> Of his fair garden and his fencit park,
> Or save belike to an infatuate tender woman:
> And then best in the dark.

This poem, spoken by Lindsay near the beginning of the play, works *as a poem* (in the way that a good song in a musical works as a song). But it also introduces the main theme of the play:

> Yet here I stand and maun contrive
> With this sole body and the brain within him
> To set myself upon ane man alive
> And turn his purposes and utterly win him.
> That coat is irrelevant:
> I will wear it nae further
> Till Armstrong be brocht

Intil the King's peace and order.
I will gang towart his house
As ane man against ane man,
And through my craft and my humanity
I will save the realm frae butchery:
Gif I can, good sir, but gif I can.

Through the language he uses, Arden has communicated very precisely the quality of Lindsay's mind. It's a mind that contains wit, intelligence, and patience. 'Do ye remember the story of the Gordian knot?' he asks. 'Aye well, there was ane emperour, and he went with ane sword and cut it. He thocht he was ane god, walken. Why in God's Name could he no be a human man instead and sit down and unravel it?'

The play is constructed round the contrast between Lindsay and Gilnockie. Lindsay, for most of the play, sees even the most violent events coolly. 'To murder ane murderer,' he says, 'is a'thegither waste.' Even when he is speaking of his mistress and expressing the urgency of his lust, he does it coolly. 'Do you find her presence ane absolute necessity?' asks the Scots Clerk. 'Absolute,' says Lindsay. 'At unpredictable intervals: but absolute.'

Gilnockie, the man Lindsay is setting out to win, is in every way Lindsay's opposite. He is rough in dress, slow of speech, uncouth and impulsive. He is not without cunning, but it's the innocent cunning of a scheming child. And there's a childlike quality in his behaviour, in his love of baubles and fancy clothes. Above all, he has a warm spontaneity which is set off against Lindsay's cool calculation. (As in *The Workhouse Donkey*, Arden doesn't identify with one rather than the other. He *presents* them and their actions, clearly and objectively.)

From the first, Arden is careful to show Gilnockie in a way that stops us from romanticizing him. When we first see him, he is in the process of carrying out a cold-blooded murder. The scene is sharp, stylized, by the use of a ballad, and very

clear. The gestures have a simple, Brechtian quality. Gilnockie
and his brothers ride out hunting, with James Johnstone of
Wamphray, a man with whom they have been at feud. They
solemnly conclude a pact, shaking hands and drinking whisky
and giving words of honour. Then, while Wamphray is
asleep, the Armstrongs take his knife, tangle up his sword,
pour whisky down the barrel of his gun, and set loose his
horse. They wake him in time to be butchered by his other
enemies, the Eliots of Stobs. As he dies, he cries, 'When ye
neist gratify your wame at Johnny Armstrang's table, speir
at him frae me, what betidit with his honour?'

What makes the scene diamond hard is the way Arden also
refuses to sentimentalize the victim. The Eliots are seeking
Wamphray because he has slept with Gilbert Eliot's daughter.
Wamphray is crude about her to the point of brutality. 'Ach
God,' he tells Armstrong, 'she is ane gat-leggit strumpet,
Johnny, and I tell you I kent it the first half-hour after!' 'Good
luck and good horsemanship to auld Gibby of Stobs and the
reeken breeks of his dochter!' he cries, drinking a toast. And
he sings drunkenly:

> Oh where are you, my lily-white love,
> Where are you, you dirty whoor?

Arden presents in a harsh, clear light both the treachery of
the Armstrongs and the crudity of Wamphray. But when
Wamphray is dead, he puts a lament into the mouth of the
'gat-leggit strumpet':

> These lips that were sae red and fat
> Will snarl across your chaps for ever
> Like the grin of a dirty rat:
> The yellow hair sae sleek and fine,
> That did illuminate your hard hasty skull
> And the deep secret dale here of your chine,
> In twa minutes has revertit
> To the draff-black bristles of a wild-wood swine.

James, ye cruel drunken lecher James . . .
To baith your woman and your godly faith
Ye were untrue.
Are ye comen, my wearie dearie,
Are ye comen, my lovely hinnie,
I will find ye a wee bracken bush
To keep the north wind frae off your ancient body.

The lament, too, is harsh, the language brutal in its realism. A woman weeps over the ugly, snarling body of a distasteful man. But the very harshness communicates strongly and directly the reality of her grief: and it comes as a cool shock when Lindsay, from the Palace at the other side of the stage, comments, 'The grief of this woman is the grief of the Common-weal of Scotland.' Lindsay has turned a concrete, particularized grief into a generalized political statement.

It is this inability to see human beings as anything other than 'The material of my craft' that limits Lindsay in his dealings with Armstrong. To Lindsay, a woman's grief is a political coin. Even where his own most personal emotions are involved, he looks for political advantage. When his mistress sleeps with Johnny Armstrong, he comments, 'I wad never claim that I had in ony way foreseen or contrivit this particular development. Gif I had, I wad hae been ane pandar. To the base lusts and deficiencies of humanity. The material of my craft, in fact. Accept them, mak use of them, for God's sake enjoy them.' And when his schemes are going badly at court, he says, 'God, gif I had her here, I wad set her to lie with Maxwell.'

No less than Musgrave or Dr Copperthwaite, Lindsay has an over-riding purpose. It expresses itself in the twists and turns of his subtle conduct, but it implies a basically simple view of human behaviour. Lindsay believes that people can always be persuaded to act rationally in their own best interests. The game lies in the setting up of situations in which other people's best interests coincide with his own aims.

But in Armstrong he comes up against a man whose conduct is not rational. 'I ken very weel what is in John Armstrang's mind,' he tells McGlass: but McGlass replies, 'There is naething in his mind but the enjoyment of man-slauchter.' 'Na, na,' Lindsay insists, 'the man desires – he yearns in his mirk bowels . . . for ane practicable, rational alternative. . . . He is ane potential magnificent ruler of his people. . . .' 'Potential, true indeed,' says the Lady, 'but unpredictable.'

It is this unpredictability that puts Armstrong outside Lindsay's comprehension. It expresses itself first in Arm-strong's relationship with the Lady. 'John,' she has said, 'ye do deserve to be ane equal man with ony King in Christianity' – and, ironically, her remark spurs on Armstrong to re-pudiate his agreement with Lindsay. 'Tell the King his Lieutenant is Armstrang. And as his Lieutenant I demand ane absolute latitude and discretion for my governance of this territory. . . . Gilbert, the neist full moon. . . . Nae further word and nae need of provocation. Gilbert, we will ride.'

And the unpredictability expresses itself again in Arm-strong's attachment to the Evangelist. 'There is nae credibility in this,' Lindsay tells him, 'and nae practicality.' But Arm-strong replies:

Hear ye this, Lindsay – your wee man Evangelist there – ye canna ca' him unpractical. We intend to extend the Kingdom of Christ . . . Whilkever direction can ensure me the best wealth and food for my people. There are monasteries in the Scots Lawlands. They tell that in Germany Martin Luther has made free the nuns and monks. And why nocht alsweel in Scotland? And Johnny will prove ane gey furious fechter, new-washit as ye see him, white in the Blood of the Lamb!

Ironically, it is Lindsay who, in a previous scene, has prevented the Evangelist from being handed over as a heretic: Lindsay's cool rationality prevents him from taking wild-wood madness seriously. But now, in the texture of the play, Arden brings the rationality and the hysteria together in contrast. 'Sir, I do salute you,' is Lindsay's formal greeting to Armstrong, and he describes himself as 'The salamander of sanity . . . betwixt the gleeds of your het fire.' But it is the hot fire that confronts him in the scene, as Armstrong and his household follow the Evangelist in a hysterical hymn, 'Again, again, brethren, assail the ears of God!' and they all cry, 'O cause, O cause our hearts to move.'

The scene has all the physical excitement of a revivalist meeting, and Lindsay's sardonic tone is swamped. And when McGlass tries to confront the Evangelist with logic, in the shape of the girl Meg, whose man Armstrong has murdered ('Whilk of these twa penitents of yours will ye accept or reject? . . . They canna be baith guests at the same Christian marriage table'), the implicit violence breaks out into action. The Evangelist snatches McGlass's gully-knife and stabs him with it.

Like the death of Sparky in *Serjeant Musgrave's Dance*, the stabbing of McGlass has about it the quality of accident. Lindsay's carefully thought-out policy founders on a sudden insane gesture by a man Lindsay had written off as an inconsequential lunatic. As McGlass staggers dying, he tells Lindsay, 'Ye did tak pride in your recognition of the fallibility of man. Recognize your ain, then, Lindsay: ye have ane certain weakness, ye can never accept the gravity of ane other man's violence.'

Confronted with the death of McGlass, Lindsay suddenly becomes aware of the reality of the game he has been playing. In a statement to the audience, he recalls his announcement at the beginning of the play:

> I did swear a great aith
> I wad wear this coat nae further
> Til Armstrang be brocht

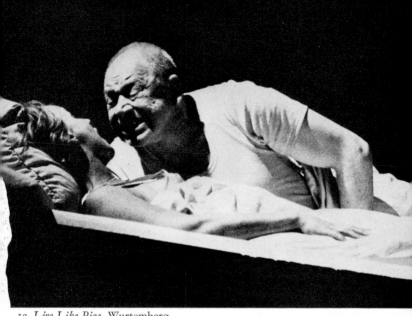

1a *Live Like Pigs*, Wurtemberg
1b *Ars Longa, Vita Brevis*

2a *Serjeant Musgrave's Dance*,
London (1959)

2b *Serjeant Musgrave's Dance*,
Paris (1963)

2c *Serjeant Musgrave's Dance*,
Minneapolis (1968)

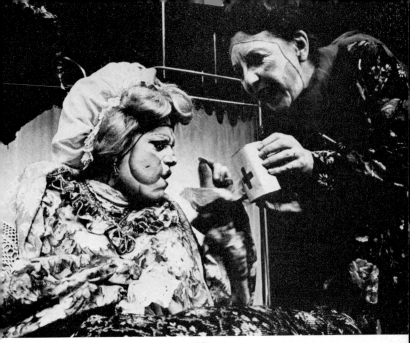

3a *The Happy Haven*, New Haven (1966)
3b *The Happy Haven*, Bristol (1960)

4a *The Workhouse Donkey*, Chichester (1963)

4b *The Ballygombeen Bequest*, Belfast (1972)

5 *Armstrong's Last Goodnight*, London (1965)

7a *The Hero Rises Up*, Nottingham/Edinburgh (1969)

6 *The Hero Rises Up*, London (1968)

7b *The Hero Rises Up*, London (1969)

8a and 8b
The Royal Pardon,
Beaford (1966)

Intil the King's peace and order.
To gang against his house
As ane man against ane man,
Through craft and through humanity –
Alas, and mortal vanity,
We are but back whaur we began.
A like coat had on the Greekish Emperour
When he rase up his brand like a butcher's cleaver:
There was the knot and he did cut it.
Ane deed of gravity. Wha daur dispute it?

The murder with which the play ends parallels the murder committed by Armstrong at the beginning. The tree against which Wamphray had been killed becomes the central image of the scene. Armstrong, who has been promised a safe-conduct by Lindsay, decks himself out in gay and ludicrous clothes, like a child dressing-up to play a game. But the game ends with his being hanged on the tree: and, ironically, before he dies, he too, like Wamphray, talks of honour. 'The King's honour, the Royal seal – but nae man can say a word against *my* honour' ('Speir him what betidit wi' his honour,' Wamphray had said before he died).

The last word in *Serjeant Musgrave's Dance* had been given to Attercliffe, and also referred to a tree, on which men were to be hanged. But the tree is seen in terms of hope, of the dropping of seed and the starting of an orchard. The last word in *Armstrong* also concerns a tree:

LINDSAY. There was ane trustless tale grew out of this conclusion –
GILNOCKIE'S WIFE. That the tree upon whilk he was hangit
  spread neither leaf nor blossom –
LADY. Nor bloom of fruit nor sap within its branches –
LINDSAY. Frae this time furth and for evermair. It did fail and
  it did wither upon the hill of Carlanrigg, as ane dry exemplar
  to the warld: here may ye read the varieties of dishonour, and
  determine in your mind how best ye can avoid whilk ane of

D

them, and when. Remember: King James the Fift, though but
seventeen years of age, did become ane adult man, and learnt
to rule his kingdom. He had been weel instructit in the
necessities of state by that poet that was his tutor.

In *Musgrave*, Arden ends by pointing to the apple which
holds a seed. Here, he points to 'ane dry exemplar'. The
withered tree is an image of the 'varieties of dishonour' that
result, says Arden, from 'the necessities of state'. And he
reminds us, in the final sentence, that the dishonour has been
perpetrated by a 'poet'.

Armstrong's Last Goodnight is about the barbarity of a
civilized, humane man – a barbarity that is forced on him by
the nature of the game he is playing. At the end of the play, a
maker of sinewy verses stands by a tree on which he has
been forced to murder a bloody murderer, and asks us to
consider his actions. And also to consider our own.

SEVEN: LEFT-HANDED LIBERTY

In 1965, the City Corporation of London commissioned John
Arden to write a play to celebrate the 750th anniversary of
the signing of the Magna Carta. Arden took the commission
very seriously. When asked if he were going to write an
historical musical as a follow-up to *The Workhouse Donkey*, he
replied that he intended to present the material as straight
and accurately as possible. But when he came to examine the
material, his eyes showed him a different picture from that
normally associated with the Magna Carta.

What the City Corporation no doubt expected was an
illustrated account of the schoolbook story of 'bad' King
John, forced by his 'good' barons to sign a charter from
which we all derive our general liberties. What Arden shows
us is that the 'good' barons' talk of liberty is merely a cloak
for tax-evasion; that the 'bad' King, although a thoroughly
dishonest politician, did dispense a rough kind of justice;

and that the charter was anyway torn up a few weeks after it was signed. And he shows us all this while presenting, with clarity, penetration and wit, the arguments of all the parties involved. In the Papal Legate's words, the play is an 'apparent spectacle of depravity, treachery and violent self-seeking' – but by the end we know precisely *why* everybody behaved as they did. *Left-Handed Liberty* is, in some ways, the most Shavian of Arden's plays. But, unlike Shaw, Arden doesn't simply set up an idea in order to knock it down. He presents each contradictory argument as urgently and cogently as he can.

Arden's two most striking inventions in the play are Pandulph, the Papal Legate, and King John himself. Pandulph plays a role familiar in Arden plays – that of the man who presents events to the audience. Arden's master-stroke lies in making this compère the spokesman of one of the most alien ideologies imaginable – that of the mediaeval, Aristotelian high cleric.

In the opening scene, Pandulph gives us his picture of the world, which he offers as if it were the only conceivable rational picture. 'Let me explain very briefly,' he says, as an opening statement in a play devoted to one of the ostensibly great moments of human progress, 'that progress in the affairs of this world has ceased to exist.' He goes on:

> That is to say, there has been progress: there have been certain cardinal events. Eve in Eden ate her fruit and then she fell and her man fell, and they discovered how naked they were. Later the Deluge, God promised it would not occur again and it did not, and after that . . . well, you may read your Bibles, it is all there.

After the Crucifixion:

> God, who had moved throughout human history, moved out at last for ever – no, not for ever. He will come once more, one day . . . but in the meantime He is not here. He has left His

representative, the Church. The Church is central to human life, as the world itself is central to the organization of the universe.

What matters in this speech is the tone. Pandulph isn't presented as a figure of fun – an absurd fuddy-duddy lost in the mists of the dark ages. He has a sharp, clear mind, and his view of the situation is also clear and precise. He demonstrates the situation on a chart:

> There is the world; the moon, and the planets, revolve in their spheres – there is the exterior sphere upon the inner surface of which the myriad stars are painted or embossed or perhaps are but little openings pricked out by God's finger to let in the light of Heaven. And here is Heaven. Hell: Purgatory: Limbo. Very good. Now, as the world is the centre of the whole created system, so Jerusalem, God's Holy City, is the centre of the world – but Jerusalem is, as you know, held by the infidel. . . . Therefore, the temporary or acting centre of the world may be taken to be Rome. . . .

Meanwhile, the Church concerns itself only with spiritual matters:

> . . . the sins and repentance of individual men, and, instructed by Our Lord, take no thought for the morrow, what raiment we should put on or what food we should consume, or how we should organize the government of nations. John, King of England, Lord of Ireland, Duke of Normandy, born Anno Domini 1167, is an anointed King and therefore requires the obedience of his subjects. That is all the Church has to say upon the matter.

The irony is implicit. A rich and powerful prelate announces that the Church has no thought for the morrow, or for food and clothing, and has no concern with politics – and then in the next sentence demonstrates a concern by announcing the Church's support of John. But the ideas are seriously and convincingly expressed. 'Not a man to make fun of,' Arden comments in his notes on the characters.

The effect of this opening speech, and of Pandulph's role as an interpreter of events, is to make us look at the action through the eyes of Rome. The result is that the story of the Magna Carta is placed in a new perspective. As Pandulph says:

Pope Innocent III has the most beautiful intellect of any man ever to have occupied the Chair of St Peter: and if he should choose to see England and the affairs of England in a correct proportion relative to the affairs of the entire world, I do not propose to run counter to his opinion. I am a native of Pisa. Archbishop Stephen . . . was (I believe) born in the County of Lincoln. There is a difference.

From the point of view of Rome, the Charter is nothing less than an attack on the Pope himself. John has announced himself as a crusader, thus making himself the Pope's man. And so when the Pope hears of the Charter, he calls it 'an agreement which is not only shameful and base, but also illegal and unjust. We refuse to pass over such shameful presumption; for the Apostolic See would be dishonoured, and the King's right injured, the English nation shamed, and the whole plan for the Crusade seriously endangered.' Practically, it is the threat to the Crusade which forces the Pope's hand. The Charter is declared 'null and void of all validity, for ever': and when the Archbishop, Stephen Langton, insists that the words on the Charter 'could no more be blotted out by King, Baron or Pope even, than I can deny the Divinity of My Saviour', Pandulph charges him with heresy, 'You attribute your own fallible words to the breath of the Holy Spirit.'

Pandulph regards the civil war which follows the tearing up of the Charter as the responsibility of Stephen Langton. 'Elimination of pockets,' he comments, 'is a craftsmanlike term. . . . It means, of course, the complete destruction of castles, houses, barns, livestock, fishing-boats, windmills, watermills, granaries, the bodies of men, the chastity of

women – I speak nothing of children.' Here, Arden is using
Pandulph's aloofness to create the equivalent of Brecht's alienation effect – he is making us see a phrase like 'elimination of
pockets' through clear, distanced eyes. But Pandulph goes on
to put the blame for these barbarities, not on John, whose
Flemish mercenaries actually carried out the atrocities, but on
the Archbishop. 'He believed he had been working, in a kind
of parenthesis, not for the Church of Christ, but for the amelioration of England – and you have heard the result.' Pandulph
also sees the French threat to invade England as a spiritual
matter: 'my instructions are precise. Curt, in fact to the point
of vulgarity. If France invades the realm of England, France
will be excommunicate and that is all there is to it.' 'They are
courting damnation,' he tells John. 'They are also courting
defeat,' John replies. 'I have a navy.'

If Pandulph sees events – and forces us to see them – from
the point of view of an alien philosophy, which believes that
nothing ever changes, and that therefore all is predictable,
John sees them from the point of view of a totally unprin-
cipled empiricist. He will use any weapon that comes to hand
to achieve his own immediate ends. His political and ideological game is played, not so much with his enemies, the
Barons, as with his ally, Pandulph. He uses Pandulph
unscrupulously, and Pandulph watches his manœuvres with
aloof disdain, scornfully allowing himself to be used, as long
as the Church benefits in the end.

Arden's King John is a mixture of Ubu Roi, Groucho
Marx, Brecht's Azdak, and Charlie Butterthwaite. He is, as
he says, unpredictable. 'Which of us,' he asks, 'dare predict
how or in what direction we are going to sin next? I have a
little mistress and last night she deceived me with a cookboy
from my kitchen. If I were the tyrannical Tiberius my loyal
barons would have you believe, I would have put her eyes out.
Instead, I went to bed with my wife.' Of St Augustine, he
comments, 'Altogether too penitent. He enjoyed his sins

while he committed them: he should have been grateful later for the pleasure he had obtained. It is never too late to give thanks.'

In his conflict with the Barons, John is altogether too clever for them, even though they have the physical strength. Waiting for him to sign the Charter, they fill the stage with their swords; but they, not him, are on tenterhooks. ('Ink, parchment, black-beetles in attendance. . . . He intends to put his seal? Or does he perhaps not so intend?') When he comes in to sign the Charter, in a casual, throwaway manner, he catches them physically by surprise. Later, when they refuse to stand on his entrance to a council at Oxford, he says, 'A relaxed posture is good for the digestion': then he calls them 'equivocating whoremongers', and, as they leap to their feet in protest, remarks, 'Good, you're on your feet. Then I can relieve mine.'

Arden presents John as an anarchic authority, a contra-diction in terms of which Arden is fully aware. He is attractive in the way that all clever stage villains are attractive. 'I never make the mistake of elevating small disputes into questions of principle,' he tells Pandulph, in the scene in which, 'under pressure and with all due calculation', he kneels and swears allegiance to the Pope. With the crown on his head ('I am glad to get it back. All my jewels are beautiful, this more beautiful than most. . . . You haven't abstracted any of the decorations, have you?'), he solemnly swears that 'as soon as I have the means and the opportunity I will lead an army to the Holy Land and redeem from the Paynim Turk, by force, the Blessed Sepulchre of Christ'. Then he looks at the cross Pandulph has hung round his neck and comments, 'Diamonds? Good. Silver-gilt. Not so good. Parsimonious, rather.' 'Make sure you keep your word,' Pandulph warns. 'The Pope is a man of honour, he expects his vassals to be likewise.' 'He has evidently little experience of the sort of vassal that I am lumbered with,' says John.

Arden makes John an engaging figure. Even in his swindles, he is outrageously self-righteous. So, he is quite capable of swearing, to two honourable men, the Archbishop and the Marshal, that he will not recruit any more mercenaries from the Low Countries; then of sending a secret recruiting message to one of his chief mercenary contractors, Hugh de Boves; and then, when he is found out, of saying brazenly to the Marshal, 'No, I can't deny it . . . it happens to be true. Now this is going to put your loyalty to quite an extensive test, is it not?'

'As for King John himself,' says Pandulph, 'that almost Oriental monster of your history books, do not forget that the records of his Household shew him to have been a tireless administrator, devoted to the pursuit of justice . . .' and immediately we are shown John, out on a luxurious picnic with his wife and mistress, pocketing the fines, but maintaining a kind of justice that keeps all the parties concerned happy.

But, Arden reminds us, this engaging figure is capable of having villages burned and people massacred. Arden shows us an attractive man, whose actions are criminal – and leaves us to make our own judgements.

The central issue of the play is not the Magna Carta itself, but John's confrontation with Pandulph. It begins in one of the opening scenes. 'I mistrust these geometrical figures,' says John, looking at Pandulph's charts of the universe. 'They are altogether too pat. If one of these circles were to have a little kink in it, thus . . . your entirely perfect mechanism would be wrecked by eccentricity.' 'Exactly so,' says Pandulph. 'If there were a kink. But a kink would be a false-hood, and a falsehood in the geometry of God is inconceiv-able.' At the climax of the play, John assaults Pandulph's logic directly.

This climax demonstrates Arden's complete confidence in his own stagecraft. In *Live Like Pigs*, he had wrapped a music-hall idiom in a naturalistic framework. In the first two acts of *Serjeant Musgrave's Dance*, the action had been tied to the stage, as if the audience didn't exist. But here, at the climax of a play, Arden is prepared to break totally with the illusionist convention. 'The Liberation of Norfolk,' says John, 'completed in mid-October 1216, is an item of military history of no great consequence whatever. So off you go – get on with it'; and the houselights go up, and he turns directly to the audience.

In the opening sentence of John's speech, Arden recalls the audience to the theatre:

> There comes a time in any stage-play, when the stage itself, the persons upon it, the persons in front of it, must justify their existence – and I think this is the time now: because on the 18th of October, I have to die, suffering from a surfeit of cider and peaches, which is a great joke, of course. . . .

Arden deliberately and consciously destroys any illusion that the rest of the play might have created. John takes off his sword – a theatre prop sword – and his crown and his mantle. 'What in fact have you seen tonight? A document signed, and nobody knew what for . . .' He picks up a copy of the Charter from behind Pandulph's chair. 'Yes: you saw me tear it up at the end of the Second Act, but I kept another copy. I always twist around, you see.'

Arden is playing with several levels of reality. Throughout the performance, we have watched an actor play a king. Now he reminds us that he is, in fact, only an actor: but he does so in a way which makes us still accept him as a king. The effect is that we are prepared to accept the Charter, not as an historic myth, nor as a prop in a play, but as a subject for consideration. When John reads us an obscure paragraph from the Charter (Paragraph 54), and then a paragraph from an historian, Dr McKechnie, explaining what the paragraph means ('The Age of Chivalry is dead – 1215. And so, of course, is Paragraph 54'), he forces us to ask questions about the Magna Carta: what exactly did it mean? what does it mean to us now?

Quoting directly from the Charter, John demonstrates that most of the clauses are completely irrelevant. ('I am not going to even try to read you what it says about the Jews, let alone attempt to argue for it.') But he calls attention to two clauses (typically, Arden throws them away):

'And no free man shall be arrested or imprisoned ... except ...' you have heard it spoken twice already. And also the other one. 'To no man will we sell or deny right and justice. ...' No detail, no precision, no temporary or feudal pettifogging ... Interpret them how you like, and agreed that they concede the Authority of the Law, not one act of injustice ... that will not be contrary to so general a clause. I gave them to you all, and all of you can use them – against the Barons, or the Bishops, or even the Crown, against the Parliaments, the Scriveners, the Catch-polls, the Beadles and the Bailiffs, the Marshals and the Serjeants – indeed, every single stone, brick, or granule of aggregate that help to build the buttresses which hold up the walls of the Temple of Authority are in peril from these clauses.

And here we are at the point where Arden's struggle with theatre form and his political commitment come together – in the image of an actor, who plays a king, deliberately stripping himself of his role and making a direct theatrical statement about the untenability of authority. For if Arden is attacking the theatre of illusion, he is attacking it *because* it is built round consistency, predictability. A joker is a joker, and a villain is a villain. Everything is neatly categorized and has its own logic: like Pandulph's circles – no kinks.

Arden asserts that it is the kinks that matter. 'Inconsistent, irregular, unreasonable,' says John. 'And that is our unique-ness. Not in our capacity for damnation or salvation nor yet in our capacity for logical rationality – though both of them are glorious: and both of them, I fear, have distorted our nature.' And he adds, 'Indeed I am inclined to think that not only are you [Lady de Vesci] unsuited to be a married woman and I to be a king, but that none of us, ever, are suited to be either.'

Left-Handed Liberty, with its ultimate denial of the theatre of illusion, is also Arden's denial of an easy, liberal rationality, based on consistency, predictability, plausibility. There are kinks in the perfect circles. But, ironically, he puts his most direct political statement into the mouth of a traditionally 'bad' king: and even at this point he holds the opposites in focus. 'Thou fool,' says Pandulph, 'this night thy soul shall be required of thee.' And in the next scene, John dies.

Left-Handed Liberty is, in many ways, an oddity. It gives the impression of not having been finally worked through. The Lady de Vesci, in particular, is altogether too pat as an image of unpredictability: and the argument is too often contained in the dialogue rather than in the action.

But the play represents Arden's last attempt for many years to come to terms with the theatre establishment. *Armstrong's Last Goodnight*, by chance, reached London later. But, after *Left-Handed Liberty*, Arden became much more involved in bringing to London a different form of theatre. It was a form which he and Margaretta D'Arcy had been involved in for several years – and which ultimately led to the controversy which surrounded the production at the Round House of *The Hero Rises Up*. But that was to be three years later, in November 1968. In the meantime, Arden almost disappeared from the London theatre scene.

3
Plays outside the Legitimate Theatre

ONE: THE BUSINESS OF GOOD GOVERNMENT

(1)

Alongside the plays conceived for full-scale professional production in London, John Arden and Margaretta D'Arcy have, from time to time, created plays intended for a very different context. These include a nativity play, produced in Somerset; a play about school, built around children's games in Kirbymoorside; and a children's play, devised with students for the Beaford Festival in Devon.

Simon Trussler, in an article in *Tulane Drama Review*, sees these plays as being designed 'rather to develop a disappearing sense of community than to put across a particular message'.[1] This seems to me to show a profound misunderstanding not only of these particular plays, but of Arden's other work as well.

In the first place, the word 'community' suggests that *all* the people in these particular localities share the same interests and aims, and that these are provided for in the Ardens' plays. In fact the Ardens see the interests of the poorer people in these communities as being at odds with the interests of the well-to-do. Increasingly in these plays they are not aiming to

[1] 'Arden's Community Dramas', *TDR*, Summer 1969, p. 182.

'develop a disappearing sense of community', but to focus attention on the conflicts and contradictions.

Secondly, the suggestion that these plays are not designed to 'put across a particular message' (in contrast, presumably, to the professional plays) implies a shifting of political attention. In fact, both the plays for the professional theatre and the plays conceived outside that theatre express very clearly the same political attitudes. In the professional plays, Arden has tried to shape the established theatre into an instrument that would express his own revolutionary vision; in these plays, created outside the profession, he tries to express that vision in an alternative form of theatre. But the vision remains the same. We can see this very clearly in the first of these plays, *The Business of Good Government*, which he and Margaretta D'Arcy produced in Brent Knoll, Somerset, in 1960.

The Business of Good Government is a nativity play. It was created for performance in a village church at Christmas. Arden himself describes the process:

> On assembling a cast, we found that the majority had never acted, and indeed had only turned up at all under pressure from the Vicar – who had apparently reassured one or two doubtful volunteers by promising that they would not be expected to *act*, merely to speak the lines as though Reading the Lesson. It was therefore essential that they should not be frightened away by the thought of having to 'build a character' in the Stanislavski sense – we concentrated instead on bringing out the meaning of their lines until, without entirely realizing it, they created from their own personalities a character, completely natural, belonging both to their own experience and to the world of the play. As rehearsals progressed I found that my lines were undergoing a number of changes – the actors' normal habits of speech reasserted themselves wherever the writing had fallen into awkwardness and pretentious phraseology, and a kind of gentle erosion of these difficult places produced in the end a simpler and stronger text than that with which we had begun.[1]

[1] Preface to *The Business of Good Government*.

In advising other groups how to stage the play, Arden comments that 'there is no substitute for imaginative improvisation to suit local conditions. . . . Generally speaking, there are no fixed rules governing such improvisations and variations – Bertholt Brecht has said, "If it works, it works." ' Arden adds, 'The one essential condition is that the meaning of the play should never be obscured.'[1]

Arden's emphasis, here, on the meaning of the play completely contradicts Simon Trussler's statement that these plays were more concerned with 'community' than with 'message'. In fact, *The Business of Good Government*, in spite of the play's apparent simplicity, has a complex political meaning. To arrive at this meaning, we need to go to the texture of the play itself.

(2)

The play begins with a traditional carol, 'I saw three ships a-sailing in', and an Angel making an announcement from the pulpit, 'Behold, I bring you tidings of great joy, which shall be unto all people. Glory to God in the highest, and on earth peace, goodwill towards men.' The opening establishes a theatre language, based on a popular tradition. Just as, in *Live Like Pigs*, Arden's form was based on traditional music-hall, so here the form is that of the even more traditional nativity play.

But having established this form, the Ardens feel free at once to cut across it. Herod picks up the last line of the Angel's rhetoric and brings it down to earth, 'Goodwill, great joy, peace upon earth – I do not believe they are altogether possible. But it is the business of good government to try and make them possible.'

From the very beginning, the Ardens have taken two elements – the traditional and the everyday – and placed them

[1] Preface to *The Business of Good Government*.

in juxtaposition. This is to be the basis of their method throughout the play. So, when the Angel quotes, 'There were shepherds, abiding in the field, keeping watch over their flocks by
night,' one of the shepherds adds, 'Ah, and a cold night – you
should say that.' The Hostess of the inn presents herself by
sweeping busily with a broom and chatting direct to the
audience, 'It's not as if they were all paying for their rooms
neither – half of 'em come here with a piece of yellow paper. . . .'
After the shepherds have sung a beautiful lullaby, full of
allusions to the mission of Jesus, the Hostess says, 'I think
they'd all had a drop too much, if you ask me.' And when the
Wise men have handed over their gifts, one of them comments,
'These people obviously have nothing to do with politics.
And I see no connection either with religion or with prophecies, or with anything else.' The Angel, who warns the
Wise Men in a dream not to return to Herod, does so by
playing the role of stage prompter.

The Ardens use the everyday, not in order to debunk the
mystery, but to place the events in a new context. 'The play is
"realist",' Arden writes, 'in that the characters stand for themselves . . . and are not intended to carry symbolical or psychological overtones. But it is also "non-realist" in that the
principal action is miraculous and accepted as such.'[1] The
Ardens aren't putting a question mark against the super-
natural events, or trying to explain them away. They accept
them as given, and incorporate them into the more general
mysteries of birth, growth, death which are at the heart of the
folk-poetry he uses in the play:

> Go to sleep, little baby, and then you will see
> How strong grows the acorn on the branches of the tree.
> How tightly it lives in the green and the brown
> But the strong storms of autumn will soon shake it down.
> The deeper it falls then the stronger will it tower
> Bold roots and wide limbs and a true heart of power. . . .

[1] *Ibid.*

(Compare this with Attercliffe's song at the end of *Musgrave*.)

But the Ardens see these mysteries in the context of real, concrete situations.

Thus, the Hostess isn't the traditional hard-hearted businesswoman associated with the phrase, 'No room at the inn'. She's a woman in a dilemma. Her rooms really are full – of people registering for the census, of Civil Servants, of the Military ('*they* don't pay neither'). 'Why should I have my premises made a scapegoat for administrative incompetence?' she asks. Her gesture of allowing Mary to go into the stable becomes one of generosity and not meanness. We understand exactly why she acts as she does.

Again, at the end of the story, we understand the actions of the Farm Girl. When Herod, in pursuit of the baby Jesus, asks, 'A man and a woman, carrying a young child. . . . Did you see them?' the Farm Girl replies, 'Yes, lord, I saw them.' There are no false heroics: but there's no condemnation of the girl either. She makes her appeal to the audience, 'They burn houses. I've seen them. . . . What about my father? He's been ill in bed all the winter. They say there's not a farm on the frontier lasts more than twenty years. . . . We have to take care.' We understand completely the girl's lack of heroism – just as we accept the miracle of the corn that has grown in an hour.

At the centre of this concrete situation is Herod himself. In the traditional mystery plays, Herod was the demon king who used to come down off the cart which formed the stage and frighten the children in the street. The Ardens present him as an intelligent politician trying to make the best of an impossible situation.

Herod explains the situation in his opening speech:

To the west, the Roman Empire. To the east, the Persian Empire. In the middle, a small country in a very dangerous position. If I lean towards the east, I am afraid of invasion from Rome; if I lean towards Rome, then I shall be called upon to fight Persia. I would prefer to choose neither. But I had to choose Rome, because Rome rules Egypt, and it is from Egypt that we buy our corn.

What choosing Rome means to Herod personally is shown immediately. 'Roman advisers in my palace,' he complains, 'Roman spies in every department . . .' and at this moment, a Secretary rises. At once Herod's tone becomes sycophantic, 'The enormous friendship and generosity shown by the Roman people to the people of Judaea can only be repaid by our continued loyalty and vigilance.'

It is this situation which governs Herod's response to the Wise Men. 'Where do they come from?' he asks casually. 'Persia,' says the Angel. 'What's this about Persia?' cries Herod in alarm – and from then on his attitude to the Wise Men is dominated by the question, 'What does the King of Persia want?'

At every step, the Ardens allow Herod to explain himself. So, after he has read the prophecies, 'And thou, Bethlehem, in the land of Judah, art not least among the cities of Judah. . .' ('The information is taken from the prophetic books of Israel. I can assure you it has been collated for me under conditions of the most exhaustive scholarship'), Herod explains, 'It was necessary to tell them. If I had pretended I had heard nothing about any prophecies, they would have found out I was lying, and in the end they would still have gone to Bethlehem. The difference would have been they would never have come back to tell me what they found.'

Herod's analysis of the political situation puts the birth of Jesus into an entirely new context:

Supposing a Son of David *should* have been born. . . . Here are the King of Persia's men, looking for what might well be a claimant to the ancient line of Israel. If Persia determines to recognize such a claimant, Rome will punish *me*. . . . They will send in an army to secure their Legitimate Interests. A Roman

E

Governor will be appointed in Jerusalem. If I am lucky, I may
be permitted to wash up in his kitchen.

At the end of his analysis, he asserts, 'I am not primarily
concerned with my own personal fortunes. The object of my
life is the integrity of my kingdom. What am I to do?'

Seen from Herod's point of view, the secret departure of
the Wise Men is a threat to the kingdom. 'Rabbit holes under
my walls. . . . The unity of this kingdom has been thrust into
peril.' Herod has, as he tells the people in a propaganda
speech, 'kept you free from war and provided unexampled
prosperity'. Now he claims the right to do what he believes to
be necessary. 'You understand,' he tells the Angel, 'I am
putting a very particular mark against my name in the history
books. . . .' And, ironically, Arden has him paraphrase a
remark usually applied to Jesus, 'It is fitting that the honour
of one man should die for the good of the people.'

The Ardens allow Herod to explain himself. But they don't
allow him an apology. They show us *why* Herod acted as he
did – but leave us to judge the actions. As Herod gives the
order to 'put to death all the children that are in Bethlehem',
he says, 'I suppose you will tell me that even this in some way
fulfils some sort of prophecy.' 'The Prophet Jeremiah,
chapter 31, verse 15,' says the Angel – and suddenly the
traditional verse brings us back to the reality of what Herod
has done, 'In Rama was there a voice heard – lamentation and
weeping and great mourning. Rachel weeping for her children
and would not be comforted, because they were not.' The
two elements, the 'miraculous' and the 'realistic', have been
synthesized. The Ardens don't comment on either. They place
them side by side and allow them to illuminate each other.

In *The Business of Good Government*, the Ardens aren't questioning the mysteries surrounding the birth of Christ from a
rationalist, agnostic point of view. But they are using the
familiar elements of a story to question the way we unthink-

ingly respond to people and events. They take out these elements, dust them, inspect them, and then rearrange them in such a way that we see them from a surprising new angle.

The shepherds heard an angel – but that didn't stop them from feeling the cold. The Hostess put Mary and Joseph in the stable – but that didn't mean she was being hard-hearted when she said there was no room. Herod killed the babies – but he too had his reasons.

Like Brecht, the Ardens, in this play, make the familiar strange, and the strange familiar. They invite us to question, not the truths of religion, which are, for them, simply a starting-point for the play (like the newspaper-cuttings which gave Arden the idea of *Musgrave*), but our own attitudes to experience.

And they do so while preserving the stylistic simplicity of a nativity play. After all Herod's explanations, we are finally left with the Corpus Christi Carol:

> Over the bed the moon shines bright:
> *The bells of Paradise I heard them ring.*
> Denoting our Saviour was born this night:
> *And I love my Lord Jesus above everything.*

TWO: ARS LONGA, VITA BREVIS

Ars Longa, Vita Brevis was first produced by Peter Brook as part of his Theatre of Cruelty programme, a season at the Lamda Theatre in 1963 in which he was exploring with professional actors the techniques suggested by Artaud. But the Ardens' play belongs much more to the world of the children at their Kirbymoorside Festival (1964) – playing games amongst the junk in the cottage garden, helping themselves to clothes from a big trunk (the clothes had come from a local gypsy encampment), and building a small stage in the lane, with flags and bunting, on which they performed their own plays – than it does to the world of Artaud, Genet and

Grotowski. The Ardens wrote the play out of children's games – and they wanted people, above all, to use it as a basis for improvisation, and developing their own ideas. They regarded the opening speech, by a headmaster, as important from a literary point of view, and also the songs with which the play ends. But for the rest, they wanted children and young people to play around the central situation – that of an art master who really wants to be a soldier, and who confuses art with battles. Used in this way, the play works on the level of schoolchildren joyfully imitating their teachers – and imagining what might be going on in their teachers' private lives.

The play opens at an annual Speech Day, when the Headmaster announces the appointment of an art master, Mr Miltiades, who, in spite of his name, is, says the Headmaster, 'exceedingly English'. In the next scene, the Headmaster interviews Mr Miltiades, who announces his creed, 'No free expression.' Teach them to draw straight lines. The Headmaster approves.

Mr Miltiades takes an art class. He begins by trying to teach them to draw straight lines, but turns it into a military drill. ('Rulers must be held in the left hand, so – and the pencil in the right. Hands up those who cannot distinguish their left hands from their right, right hand up. Left hand up. No. Try again, smarter. Left hand up. Right hand up. . . . NO! Left, right, left, right, left! It is evident you are in need of drill. . . . All out here, quickly.') When the Headmaster comes in, the children are fighting a battle and Mr Miltiades is standing in the middle shouting, 'Kill each other kill each other kill each other KILL!' (In a production with Girl Guides directed by Margaretta D'Arcy at Kirbymoorside, the Headmaster shouted, 'What do you think you're doing, Mr Miltiades?' 'Teaching them to draw straight lines, Headmaster,' came the reply.)

Back at home, Mr Miltiades quarrels with his wife. He

joins the Territorial Army, and goes for Sunday manœuvres
in the woods. During the manœuvres, they dress up as trees:
but the Headmaster, out hunting with the school governors,
shoots Mr Miltiades dead.

The story has a surrealist, anarchic quality that springs
from a sharp, child's-eye view of social institutions. This
child's-eye view cuts right through social pretensions. 'It
has been a very good year,' says the Headmaster in his Speech
Day report, 'and we have all made a lot of money.' It's the
sort of truth that lies behind Speech Day reports, but is never
actually spoken. When the governors go hunting, they say,
'And upon a Sunday too, what special pleasure it is to be able
to shoot animals and birds instead of going to church.' After
her husband's death, Mrs Miltiades says, 'Now I can have all
those things that I was unable to enjoy before because of the
poor pay of the teaching profession.' The simplicity is very
accurate.

But behind the simplicity, paradoxes are at work. So,
in his interview with the Headmaster, Mr Miltiades, who
hates free expression, expresses very freely his enthusi-
asm for 'Squares, cubes, tetrahedrons, parallelograms,
triangles, cones, conic sections, hexagons. . . .' The list pours
from his lips as if it were a lyric poem. He believes in discipline – but he turns his art lesson into a chaotic battleground.
He believes in authority – 'have I not always commanded?'
he asks his wife. 'My God, you are a Prussian,' she replies,
'and I worship you, my treasure.' But when he asks for 'a
large pot of Indian tea, a small jug of milk, a medium jug of
hot water, seven lumps of sugar, and three toasted teacakes',
she simply replies, 'You shall not have them.' 'What about the
discipline?' he cries, when the Territorial Officer invites him
to 'Enjoy yourself, improve yourself, learn a trade and learn
a skill.' 'Oh well, of course we have to have it,' says the
Officer apologetically; but the Art Master cries, 'Of course,
of course, I want it!' He turns inside out the conventional

reasons for joining the professionals, and begs for the harshness the Officer would prefer to forget.

The two final poems sum up, in direct terms, the contradictory images of the play. The Territorials have dressed up as
trees – the scene should have all the quality of a child's game
of cowboys and Indians. They are very clearly *pretending* to be
trees, and the Headmaster also talks about pretending, '*I*
know they are men, but I do not wish these others to know
that too, because it would be a good joke to see how long it
takes them to tell the difference between a tree, a Territorial,
and a deer.' The Headmaster shoots a pretend bullet at the
man he pretends to think is a deer, who is pretending to be a
tree – and the man steps forward, in the style of an Elizabethan actor summing up his own career:

> Oh delight of my life
> I did not dream in vain
> I put on the khaki to stifle my pain
> I went to the manœuvres
> But endured the coarse laughter
> Of those who believed that the life of the soldiers
> Was no more for glory, ferocity and steel
> But was only the achieving of a poor bourgeois skill.
> Technology is confounded and art takes its place:
> For here I have received a real bullet in my face.
> Hardihood and discipline,
> Straight lines and repression
> Have today found their old true expression:
> I die for my duty and I die with a smile
> The Territorial Army has proved itself real.

Miltiades gets enjoyment out of pain; he finds free expression in straight lines and discipline; and sees art as destruction.
Having received a pretend bullet (which he says is real) in
his face, he pretends to die.

His widow, lamenting and enjoying herself at his funeral,
takes up the theme of 'straight lines':

I shed a tear upon his bier
Because to me he was ever dear.
But I could not follow him in all his wishes
I prefer the quick easy swimming of the fishes
Which sport and play
In green water all day
And have not a straight line in the whole of their bodies.

The play ends with an invitation to celebrate: but the problem in production is always to make the celebration happen. The only time I've ever seen it take off was when I performed the play with a group of actors in a pub in Bradford and had a rock group ready to take over as soon as the play had ended. The whole audience began spontaneously to join in the dancing.

And it's this kind of spontaneity that *Ars Longa, Vita Brevis* is ultimately about.

THREE: THE ROYAL PARDON

Of the three plays linked with particular localities, *The Royal Pardon* is both the longest and the most ambitious. It was put together by the Ardens and a group of students for performance as part of the Beaford Festival in 1966. Like *Ars Longa, Vita Brevis*, it presents a child's-eye view of the world: its characters are people *playing*. But it's more rich and complex than *Ars Longa, Vita Brevis*, and takes further the exploration of the theme of the connection between authority and anarchy.

The Royal Pardon tells the story of the adventures of a group of strolling players who fall in with a deserter from the wars in Flanders. The deserter, Luke, has been arrested by the Constable, but he escapes, hitting the Constable over the head. He takes refuge with the players – which means that throughout the play the group is pursued by the Constable. At the beginning of the play, the players are condemned by

the ferocious Constable as vagrants; but they receive a
pardon, inviting them to play in a competition organized by
the King. The winners of the competition are to represent
English theatre at the wedding of the King of England's son
to the King of France's daughter.

The players won't let Luke perform, because he's not a
professional actor; so he becomes stage carpenter, and the
play wins the royal competition because the King likes the
set. Over in France, the French actors dope the English group
to make sure they won't win the prize. But Luke isn't allowed
to eat with the actors. He has brought his own sandwiches,
and so isn't drugged. He succeeds in rousing the girl in the
group, and together they perform all the parts in the play
within the play. The Constable blunders in and becomes
involved with the performance.

From the beginning, the Ardens make it clear that they are
playing with ideas about theatre. A group of actors is heard
singing behind a curtained booth:

> Sun and moon and stars and rainbow
> Drum and trumpet, tambourine,
> A greedy king or a haughty beggar
> A virgin slut or a painted queen –
> Put your boots on, mask your faces
> Heave your cloaks and swing your swords,
> Laugh and weep and stamp with anger
> Kick your jigs and strut the boards,
> All is painted, all is cardboard,
> Set it up and fly it away.
> The truest word is the greatest falsehood,
> Yet all is true and all in play . . .

The song announces the theme of the play: truth is to be
explored through the falsehood of theatre. When the actors
appear, they are clearly actors, with masks and false noses: in
the Ardens' own production the actors wore their robes over
blue jeans and basketball boots.

In this opening scene, a number of theatrical conventions are established. A clown comes on and is attacked by a dragon, who is obviously a girl. He splits his breeches. 'Why, I was going to give you a prologue,' he says, Frankie Howerd style. The actors play out, in verse, the story of George and the Dragon and the Clown splits another pair of breeches.

When the Constable appears, he makes the kind of speech that would be expected of a policeman in a children's radio programme such as *Toytown*. 'Twice, no less, was breeches mentioned, and each time they was removed: to the scandal of the populace. Whatever you might get away with in London, we do *not* allow that sort of thing round here. . . . Why – children might have been present.' Since the play is meant for children, the Ardens are playing games with the audience. The actors make contact with the real children in the audience by inviting them to share an in-joke.

The same thing happens when Luke, the soldier, is introduced. He talks at once to the audience, 'Tearing his pants off – *twice*! Well, did anybody laugh at it – did you? I didn't.' Since the children will have laughed if the Clown has done his job properly, Luke's remark, like the Constable's, is toying with different levels of reality.

Luke proposes a different kind of entertainment. 'And what about St George?' he says. 'There was a man, if they'd had the intelligence to look out a proper play about him . . .' The Ardens, having set up a pantomime in which a clown splits his breeches, allow Luke the comment that such a play isn't 'proper'. To Luke, a 'proper' play is a heroic drama:

> His sword was strong, his heart was clear;
> Inside his stomach he knew the claws of fear.
> But he fought them first, and then he fought again. . .

In these opening scenes, the Ardens are establishing the same kind of child's-eye view that they offered in *Ars Longa, Vita Brevis*. Throughout the play they offer the same kind of incongruous, but accurate images. So, the Constable approaches Luke very formally and politely. 'I'm afraid I have no alternative but to ask you,' he says, 'as a purely routine matter, just to answer a few questions, you understand, and to assist the police, and finally, to accompany me, and my subordinate here, with as little fuss as possible, into the lock-up.' The language is mock-legalistic – but the Constable punctuates it by punching Luke in the stomach, hitting him across the neck, and twisting his arms behind his back. The comedy comes from the contrast between the formality of the Constable's speech and the violence of his behaviour. It's a child's-eye view of what a policeman arresting a thug is like.

Again, a policeman makes an official arrest – but he has to do so in his underpants, because his wife can't thread a needle to mend his trousers. The mysterious wizard, Merlin, is absurdly played by the Clown – who once again splits his breeches. An actor tries romantically to pluck a rose from a trellis – and the whole trellis falls down. The King of England gives the actors three and fourpence for expenses to take them to France – but he gives the Constable fifty guineas to pursue them. (The Constable has accused them of attempted murder, which is, apparently, much more serious than the real thing.)

The gags are used primarily because they're funny and entertaining – but all of them are involved with the illusory world of the travelling players. It seems quite logical that in this strange world, both the King of England and the King of France should warn their respective offspring not to fall in love with each other, because they're only marrying for political convenience: and it seems equally logical when the Prince tells the Princess:

> I shall swallow you whole
> If only for a while:
> Let us both tell our children
> That we ate and we were full.

At the climax of the play, the Ardens explore the various levels of illusion in an extraordinarily complex way. The Constable, in his search for Luke, has disguised himself as a gendarme, and he comes upon the Princess, who is laughing hysterically at the failure of the French play. The Constable decides that she is Luke, disguised as a princess.

'His demeanour . . . is clearly uncontrolled,' says the Constable, speaking about the laughing princess. 'See, he rolls about and gnaws the backs of his hands as though in the torments of justified remorse. . . . Watch me – this is crafty,' the Constable goes on. He creeps up behind the Princess, pulls his hat down over his eyes, and whispers in a false, high-pitched voice:

> Blood on a bottle and a hole in his head
> But strange to say he was not dead.

When the Princess stares at this apparent maniac in bewilderment, the Constable says, 'Pale as death, you give away your very soul.' And when she protests, in French, this apparent gendarme says, 'Jabber jabber jabber – You can't deceive me. You're as English as I am.'

The scene is all about conventions of theatre. Is a girl, with her hands clapped to her mouth, laughing, or showing 'justified remorse'? Does a facial expression 'give away your very soul'? How do we interpret what we see?

The scene reaches a climax of misunderstanding when the Prince comes in. The Constable is pulling at the Princess's hair, 'I said take it off. And we'll have off that gown and all. . . .' The Prince interferes, pointing to his coronet – 'What's this – upon my head?' 'Cardboard,' says the Constable. 'You can't fool me. I know a theatrical property when I see one. And don't you threaten me with your old wooden sword. . . . Ow-hey-up, that's sharp.'

The point is that the sword *is* wood: but the Constable and the Prince agree that it's a real one. And the coronet *is* a theatrical property: you can see that it's made of cardboard. But when it's knocked off the Prince's head, it falls to the ground with a clang.

The scene is wildly funny – but through the comedy a serious point is made. Earlier, Luke has talked about the war in Flanders. 'We met fever, we met starvation, pouring rain and flooded country. . . . I got a blow from a partisan on the corner of my forehead. . . . When I recovered my senses I found myself alone among a great field of dead men. . . . There are inevitable deeds have been performed in Flanders this last year that no decent man should inquire after.'

At the climax of the play, the Ardens, through a series of gags, are questioning what is real. The actor is only playing with a toy sword: but the toy sword can kill. The soldiers in Flanders are only dressed up actors: but the games they are playing are games of real death.

As the Constable advances with his sword on the Princess, Luke says, 'It's all right. . . . It's all under control.' He takes his own crown off. 'Cardboard.' And he orders the Prince and the Princess to take theirs off too. 'They're all three of them cardboard – so put them down.' Then he sings:

> Cardboard and paper and patches and glue
> Pleated and crumpled and folded in two
> With a pair of white fingers and a little bit of skill
> We make a whole world for the children to kill. . . .

Through their games with illusion, the Ardens have, in the end, created a joyful, anarchic world. As the Constable, who has been turned to stone by an actress wearing a gorgon's mask, finally says:

> It is no use to be a policeman
> The force of anarchy wins all the time. . . .

Paradoxically, the representative of Law and Order has reduced everything to chaos: it is the deserter who has put everything to rights.

The Royal Pardon is essentially a children's play. It looks at events with a child's eye. But the Ardens don't make the mistake of patronizing children by talking down to them. They assume that children have wit and imagination, and so they take a complex, political theme, and present it in terms of a magic, toy theatre.

The result is a play that is enjoyable on many levels to children and adults alike.

4

The Hero Rises Up

(1)

The Royal Pardon was produced in 1966. The Ardens' next major play, *The Hero Rises Up*, reached the Round House in 1968. But in the meantime the Ardens had become involved with making a film in Oughterard in Ireland; they had worked with a political theatre group, CAST, on a play at the Unity Theatre, and had spent some time at New York University, at the invitation of Conor Cruise O'Brien. During this period they were consciously and actively extending, in a political direction, the kind of activities they had sparked off at Brent Knoll, Kirbymoorside and Beaford.

In New York, for example, they staged a day-long event. At the time of *The Workhouse Donkey*, Arden had wanted to write a play that could go on for thirteen hours, with people wandering in and out to see the episodes that particularly interested them. A similar idea formed the framework for the New York event.

The event was built around a combination of military game and television serial. On entering the hall, the audience was invited to join in a game. This involved military drill and mock combat. The television serial occurred at regular intervals throughout the day. It was about a hill-billy family – a perfectly normal television serial family: except that the daughter had a slight peculiarity. Every time she made love, she gave birth to an H-bomb. Grandma encouraged promiscuity, with the result that by the end of the play she was flying around over Washington and controlling the world. The day involved several other events, including a straight lecture by Conor Cruise O'Brien.

Towards the end of the day, an emotional situation began to develop. Slides of concentration camps were shown; some of the audience began singing Jewish folk-songs; the feeling in the hall became very violent.

At this point, Arden himself appeared on the stage. He had, he said, been commissioned by the CIA (whose backing of student societies was becoming notorious) to instigate a Vietnam show in order to find out just how serious was the dissent among the NYU students. As the show was 'getting out of hand', he was prepared and able to close it down. He proved this by having all the lights switched off.

The revolutionary fervour in the hall suddenly withered away. After which Arden himself broke the law, not in any Musgrave revivalist sense, but coolly, by stepping on to the American flag as, in Arden's own words, 'a quiet statement of civil disobedience to contrast with all the over-excited stuff that had been going on before'. Talking about the event afterwards, Arden commented: 'It fell into a state of turbulence in the American mind.'

Back in London, and working with CAST, the Ardens wrote their most consciously propagandist play to date, *Harold*

Muggins is a Martyr. It is also one of their least successful. The play is about the employees of a broken-down old café, which is taken over and modernized by a set of gangsters; they rebel against both their boss, Harold Muggins, and the gangsters who are running him. At the end of the play they sing:

> By God we've got him frightened!
> And then we carry on from there.
> There are more of us than there are of him
> It stands to reason we shall win.

– but the song is little more than expression of pious hope. In fact, Arden's dramatic sense of opposites conflicts with the simple line the play demands, and the result is neither one thing nor the other. Ironically, the most successful scene has no direct connection with the political message. It's a strip scene. One of the gangsters who is transforming the Muggins' café introduces a stripper. With great excitement, Muggins asks her to strip in front of him. She does so, beautifully but coldly, showing him, and the audience, an attractive body. But when she's completely naked, Muggins simply says, disappointed, 'Is that all?' Arden succeeds, in this scene, in doing what he tried to do in the night-club scene in *The Workhouse Donkey* – in making us aware both of the beauty of the girl's body, and of the pointlessness and frustration of commercialized sex. In the year of the tasteful, glamorized, discreetly-lit nudity of *Hair*, the scene made a clear, simple comment on the use of nudity in the theatre.

The *Harold Muggins* play was produced in May 1968: but soon the Ardens were working on a much more ambitious project – the musical about Trafalgar which had been in their mind for several years. It finally emerged, not on Broadway, for which it had been originally conceived, but as a home-made show, created by himself and Margaretta D'Arcy and presented at the Round House under the auspices of the Institute of Contemporary Arts. The show was a great popular success. It packed the Round House for four nights – and was received by the critics with disdain. It marked the climax so far, of the Ardens' confrontation with the conventional theatre establishment.

(2)

The Hero Rises Up is, as the title suggests, a play about a hero. The hero is Nelson, a mutilated midget who won the Battle of Trafalgar. The play is written in the style of a tuppence-coloured nineteenth-century melodrama, with all the gusto, energy and incongruity that such a form implies. Only into the melodrama has been injected a detached and ironic intelligence, which uses the form both to celebrate and to question an English myth.

The play tells the story of the main events in Nelson's life from the 'liberation' of Naples to his death at Trafalgar. Some of the events are public, others are private. The public events include the execution of the revolutionary Caracciolo, in Naples; Nelson's heroic return to London; the Battle of Copenhagen, with the celebrated episode of the telescope to the blind eye; and the Battle of Trafalgar itself. The private episodes involve Nelson's romance with Lady Hamilton, and his separation from his wife, Fanny. But in all the events, the public and private lives of Nelson are inextricably entangled. So, commenting on the execution of Caracciolo, Allen, Nelson's servant, sings:

> Yet he does not know and she does not know
> Why the politics of Naples disturb them so:
> Yet sure if they did, they would think it wrong
> That to get them to bed a man must hang.

The Battle of Copenhagen is mixed up with a champagne celebration of the birth of Nelson's illegitimate child; and the Battle of Trafalgar is preceded by the writing of Nelson's

bequest to the nation. One of the central political episodes –
an orgy of anti-intellectual, counter-revolutionary book
burning by Nelson's hosts in London – is fused with the
private battle for Nelson that is going on between Fanny
(with her talk of the kitchen-pump) and Emma Hamilton
('get her legs in the air'). One of the Ardens' central themes is
this link between the public actions and the private feelings
of the hero.

The style of *The Hero Rises Up* is the most consciously
Brechtian and anti-illusionist that the Ardens have developed.
From the mock-scholastic opening, with its deliberately
pedantic comments on heroes, ending with an appeal to the
audience to imagine the sexual congress of Nelson and Emma
('I want to hear you all breathing very hard'), through to the
laconic climax of the Battle of Trafalgar ('When he died he
asked Hardy to kiss him: and he did. I think he would have
asked anyone to kiss him – except his own wife. He was buried
in St Paul's'), the Ardens constantly and deliberately remind
us that we are watching a piece of theatre. The characters
present themselves two-dimensionally ('If you don't know
who I am, you ought to be ashamed of yourselves, God
damn your eyes,' shouts Nelson, when he first appears,
bursting through a screen); they harangue each other in scraps
of operetta and doggerel; placards break up scenes at the
most conventionally dramatic moments; much of the story is
told in third-person narrative. And there is a conscious
rejection of conventional 'dramatic' opportunities. So, the
whole story of the Battle of Copenhagen is told with Nelson
and Hardy standing at one side of the stage and Admiral
Parker at the other. It's only after the victory is won that the
Ardens offer us a visual image. The wounded are carried on
stretchers across the stage, since that's what battle is really
about.

This stylization leaves the Ardens free to show very clearly
the basic contradictions of the story. Take, for example, the

'liberation' of Naples. It's demonstrated through the use of a
sea-shanty. As the ships weigh anchor, the sailors sing:

> King George's ships are on the tide
> Sing ho for liberty
> With our rows of guns on every side
> We've come to make you free.

But as the song goes on the words become increasingly
ironic:

> In Naples city there was a brawl
> Ho for liberty
> But Nelson he didn't mind that at all
> He'd come to make 'em free.
>
> He ordered in his red marines
> Sing ho for liberty
> And he smashed them all to smithereens
> All for to make 'em free.
>
> We caught the chief of all the gang
> Sing ho for liberty
> And we beat him down with many a bang
> We meant to make him free.
>
> We tied his arms with a length of twine
> Sing ho for liberty
> And we dragged him up at the end of a line
> That's how we made him free.

The song is gay and jaunty. Its *style* evokes all the clichés
of brave, independent English sea-dogs, sailing the oceans of
the world in defence of their own hard-won freedom: but in
its content it tells the story of an act of repression. The 'chief
of all the gang' is the leader of a libertarian revolution in
Naples: he is hanged, in the name of order, by an admiral
who has himself disobeyed instructions – and the hanging is
carried out by men with the songs of liberty on their lips.

The Ardens use a traditional style of sea-shanty to comment directly on a political contradiction.

Again, there is a scene in which the Ardens use a classical charade to point out the moral hypocrisies of the period. The victor of the Nile – or, as his stepson, Nisbet, puts it in a Brechtian song, the governor of a floating gaol of wood, the fleet – has returned to general acclaim in London and has gone with his wife and the Hamiltons to a party, at which there is a royal guest. The hosts and the royal guest snub Emma Hamilton, until it's suggested that she should perform her 'attitudes'. ('I'm looking forward to these Attitudes,' says the royal guest – 'dancing naked on the tables!')

The Ardens use the charade as a step in the story (Emma is luring Nelson away from Fanny); as a way of giving information about Emma herself; and as an image of the contradictions of an apparently heroic era. So, Sir William Hamilton, in the middle of the stage, hands Emma the props to form classical attitudes ('The Spirit of Peace aware of the threat of Strife') and Emma utters noble sentiments:

> But hist, hark, where all has been serene
> I hear the rumbling thunder and the lightning flash doth gleam.

But, standing at the two front corners of the stage, framing the action, Nelson's servant, Allen, and Emma's mother, Mrs Cadogan, tell in raucous verses the story of Emma's career as a tart:

> Her naked limbs being on display
> On my old knees I knelt to pray.
>
> Upon her own knees she did tumble:
> Her pretty little bum was pink and humble.

The contradictions are both visual and verbal. The heroic visual image, classical in form, is distanced physically by the presence of Allen and Mrs Cadogan: and in the same way the heavy metre and rhetoric of Emma's verses are counterpointed by the jaunty and earthy rhythms of the mocking song. The climax is reached when Emma draws Nelson into her charade:

> We crown the Ruler of the Sea:
> Old Neptune bows on bended knee . . .
> Each wave precurrent now must roar –
> All hail all hail, the Victor of the War!

while Allen comments:

> So old and pale her husband grew
> She could not teach him all she knew,
> He would not rise for rub nor scrub
> He lay like flannel in the old wash-tub . . .

Finally, the image of the 'classical attitudes' itself breaks down, as the guests become a jigging chorus and 'the party threatens to become a riot'. Fanny 'suddenly thrusts herself forward' and says, 'Horatio – the charades are now over – will you please take off that silly crown!' As in *The Royal Pardon*, the levels of illusion are all mixed up. Nelson has been crowned in charade. But he *is* the victor of the Nile. Or was that victory, too, only a charade? The dead sailors are real, even though Emma Hamilton, in an unreal verse, says they are.

The scene of the classical attitudes is typical of the Ardens' method throughout *The Hero Rises Up*. On the one hand there's all the genuine panache and extravagance of a heroic melodrama: and on the other hand, there's the cool, ironic distancing of the events shown. The panache comes mainly from Nelson himself:

> I broke the rules of warfare
> And the nation did forgive:
> But there was no forgiveness when
> I broke the rules of love.

and from Emma Hamilton. ('Nelson: rise up! You are not here to repine for what no man could have been expected to achieve. Bonaparte you did not kill, but the whole French fleet of line-of-battleships a few days later in Aboukir Bay you burnt and sank and blew into ludicrous fragments.') The coolness comes from Allen, from Mrs Cadogan, but, above all, from Nelson's stepson, Nisbet.

From the beginning, the Ardens use Nisbet as a way of bringing into a different focus the heroic clichés of Nelson's career. Nisbet first appears accompanied by a placard that reads: CAPTAIN NISBET'S DISSENT. His first words are, 'No no no! A wife is a wife and his wife was my mother. I am not going to permit them to shovel her under the orlop deck.' And throughout the play there are many other aspects of Nelson's career that Nisbet refuses to allow to be shovelled away. He announces his role in his first song:

> I was there and I saw it, the start of your story
> Was not at any moment of victory and joy:
> But a time of confusion and bloody-minded treason
> When the honour of Old England had wilted away ...

And at the end of the Battle of Copenhagen, when Nelson, by putting his telescope to his blind eye, has won one of his greatest victories, Nisbet comments, as the dead and wounded seamen are carried across the stage, 'Yet even as the result of this kind of a shambles we do occasionally find ourselves at peace.'

It is into Nisbet's mouth that the Ardens put two of the most anti-heroic songs in the play. They form the introductions to the second and third acts.

The first is accompanied by the placard, THE HERO'S TRIUMPHANT RETURN. 'Upon Lord Nelson's arrival in London they filled every street with carnival!' Nisbet tells us.

> And what came they out into the wilderness to see? The man who hanged Caracciolo? God help us, out of one hundred in that multitude there might possibly be a single informed person who had at least a notion of who Caracciolo was.

> For had they all known who he was –
> Being ragged dirty British skin-and-bone –
> It is just possible they would have cried
> For a bold Caracciolo of their own.

Nisbet goes on to comment, directly, on the social background against which Nelson's victories were won:

> A little island in our island home
> Is made of stone: they call it Newgate Gaol.
> We have a floating island made of wood:
> The fleet that won the Battle of the Nile.
>
> If you don't like the one, then try the other:
> The King and Parliament have made quite sure
> That angry ragged men have no third choice –
> We're on an island and we are at war.
>
> The noble Governor of Newgate Gaol
> Is not acclaimed by thousands in the street:
> But when the Victor of the Nile comes home
> Red roses bloom beneath his sacred feet.

The song says things that aren't usually mentioned, when people think of Nelson's victories. The image of the fleet as a floating Newgate Gaol puts the Battle of the Nile into a totally different perspective, and forms an ironic background to Nelson's remark immediately afterwards, 'The people, of all sorts and conditions, have rendered us a great welcome, which has moved me to tears.'

Nisbet's song at the beginning of the third act (PEACE: AS CREATED BY THE TREATY OF AMIENS, 1802) plays a similar, distancing role. It is a song about the whole purpose of a 'decade of war': Nisbet sings it in his officer's uniform, but with a civilian coat over his arm:

> The bare-arsed hordes of hungry Frenchmen
> Stand exactly as they were:
> The Kings of Europe have not destroyed them,
> The Poor of Europe are just as poor.

The crowned Kings of Royal Europe
Still sit proudly on their thrones:
The furious French have not destroyed them,
The furious French have a King of their own.

They did not want him nor expect him,
They do not know yet that he is there:
They know he is a successful general,
They know he has not lost the war.

But I've lost mine and I feel no guilt for it,
The blue and the gold I do discard –
If I were a gaudy and jingling hero
I would no doubt take it very hard . . .

War, says Nisbet, has changed nothing. The Kings are as powerful, the poor are as poor. The revolutionary French are soon to have another King, created by the war itself. But there are people for whom peace means, literally, a 'lost war': the phrase takes on a new meaning – the 'gaudy and jingling' heroes have literally 'lost' their war, and, therefore, the point of their lives. Nisbet demonstrates the lost war by taking off his gaudy officer's coat and putting on a civilian coat instead. And then, at once, Arden shifts perspective again. Having just lamented, in song, the plight of the poor, Nisbet tells Hardy, 'I have set myself up in business, you see, and I am happy to tell you I look like making a great deal of money.' For him, the 'lost war' means a transformation from a gaudy hero into a successful shopkeeper.

The Ardens' most original idea in the whole of the play is to see Nelson's greatest triumph through the eyes of this disenchanted, alien figure. The clichés of Trafalgar are common knowledge: the 'Nelson touch', 'England Expects', 'Kiss me, Hardy . . .'. The Ardens put them into the ironic mouth of Nisbet:

NISBET. He called this the 'Nelson touch' – it was like an electric shock. Some shed tears, all of them approved. It was new, it was singular, it was simple.

The words are Nelson's own. Spoken in the third person by Nisbet, they become cool, sardonic:

NISBET. Then he gave out a signal:
NELSON. England confides that every man will do his duty.
NISBET. But they couldn't hang up 'confides' without using too many flags so –
HARDY. So what about 'expects'. I suggest to you 'expects', my lord, that entails no more than three flags.
NISBET. So with three flags it was done.

The Ardens use Nisbet to give a precise and detailed description, both of the nineteenth-century form of sea-warfare:

The bulkheads are removed throughout the ship. . . . The Surgeon and his mates, in the lowest level of the ship, prepare their make-shift operating theatre, laying out seamen's chests for amputations and all the tools that will be needed. . . . To encourage the men who are to die the band of the Royal Marines commences to play. . . .

and of Lord Nelson's battle-plan:

Bear in mind the practical disadvantage of Lord Nelson's plan of battle. As the British fleet in two columns advances slowly towards the enemy, only the small guns in the bows of the leading ships can fire. But the entire larboard armament of the Frenchmen and Spaniards is able to be brought to bear. Their roundshot and chainshot whirl continually through our rigging: their canister-shot ploughs among the sailors on our decks, time and again and time and again and time and again: and the men must endure it. They endure it for hours, so feeble is the wind and so cunctatious is the slow encroachment of the fleet. . . .

Nisbet talks at length about the suffering and endurance of the men. But when the climacteric moment of Nelson's heroic death finally comes, it is thrown away in an aside.

By forcing us to see Nelson through Nisbet's eyes, the Ardens place their hero in an ironic framework and make us contemplate him sardonically. But the greatness of the play lies in the fact that as well as 'placing' and scrutinizing Nelson, they communicate to us all his charm, his bravery, his passion, and above all his audacious disregard for authority and convention – all those qualities that made him the hero, not simply of the mob and the court, but of the seamen for whose deaths he was responsible. The Ardens don't satirize Nelson, or cut him down to ordinariness. They make him a genuine hero to be celebrated – and at the same time ask us if heroes like this are what we need.

Nisbet himself sums up the ambiguity in his final speech, made beside the gilded marine-chariot that is to carry Nelson, Fanny and Emma to the Gods:

> Caracciolo lost his life
> Old Hamilton could not keep his wife:
> Equality, Fraternity, and so on never came:
> And where we were then, now we are just the same.
> This Hero fought for us 'gainst all the odds:
> It did not help. So: now he's with the Gods.
> We are all gathered here to send him off.
> It would be better not to scoff.
> We needed him: he did what we required:
> He goes to heaven: that is his reward.
> All of us, for whom he died,
> Have no reward, because we never tried
> To do without him on our own.
> Here is a ship-shape chariot: let it be his throne.

The play ends extravagantly, with Nelson and his Ladies being hauled up to heaven:

> For what the world may think or say –
> We damn the world – We lie and play
> We are for ever flown away,
> With a fal lal lal la la la la. . . .

But the man who does the hauling, Allen, the servant, remains in his working clothes. And when Nelson shouts,

'You are promoted, Bosun. That make you happy?' he remains, as the Ardens put it, expressionless.

The Ardens leave the contradictory images to the end: and, like Brecht, in this most Brechtian of the Ardens' plays, allow the audience to make its choice.

(3)

This, then, was the play that the Ardens offered to the public at the Round House in November 1968. But the circumstances in which it was produced were as contradictory as any Arden play could be.

The play was sponsored by one of the keystones of the artistic establishment, the ICA, with its headquarters in the Mall. The ICA was at that time being run by one of the leading apologists of Brecht in this country, Michael Kustow. Kustow had worked for a year with France's leading revolutionary director, Planchon, and he was trying to use his position at the ICA to push the institution in a more popular direction. While he was there, he changed the content of ICA programmes considerably. He put on an exhibition of comics, found a home for Bruce Lacey's sex-machines, and brought the People Show and Manfred Mann into the Mall. But what he failed to do was change, to any meaningful extent, the make-up of the audience. So when, for example, after being approached by Margaretta D'Arcy on behalf of America's most genuinely political theatre group, the Bread and Puppet, he made a hall available for them near the ICA, the Bread and Puppet themselves found the audience totally unappreciative – whereas when the same group went to a hall near the Oval, they got exactly the response they were hoping for.

Kustow's commissioning of *The Hero Rises Up*, which had been hanging around for several years, was one of his serious attempts to encourage political theatre. But while the Ardens were working on the production, they found themselves increasingly at odds with the ICA bureaucracy. In the end, the Ardens threw open the Round House, and let audiences in free. At one time it looked as if the actors weren't going to get paid.

In an article in the *Tulane Drama Review*, Simon Trussler implies that the Ardens wanted a rough, messy production. This is to misunderstand completely the remarks the Ardens make in their preface to the play about not wanting things to be done 'properly'. By 'properly', the Ardens didn't mean 'professionally': they meant with decorum – and decorum is the last quality the Ardens' play demands. The Ardens contrast the 'rectilinear' approach of the Romans who invaded Britain, with the 'curvilinear' attitude of the native Celts. In the preface to the play they write:

> This play is about a man who was, by accident of birth and rearing, committed to a career governed by the old Roman 'rectilinear' principles. He himself was of asymmetrical 'curvilinear' temperament to an unusually passionate degree. But the English soon discovered how to handle him. He was *done properly*: wasted his extraordinary energy, courage, and humanity upon having men killed (in the end himself killed): and then finally was installed as a National Monument. We meant to write a play which need not be *done properly*.

But they didn't want to write a play which would be done badly. And if, in the final production, the lighting was bad, the seating chaotic and many of the scenes unable to be seen or heard properly, this wasn't because the Ardens wanted it that way. It was because effective communication between the Ardens and the ICA had broken down. Afterwards, the Ardens were convinced that they'd been denied the co-operation necessary to make such a large-scale undertaking work. As it turned out, the play was a popular success in spite of and not because of the management.

But this wasn't the end of the paradoxes. The Ardens had rightly decided that the play should go on in the Round

House, rather than Carlton House Terrace, because, over the last few years, the Round House had become the home of the young underground. *The Hero Rises Up* was created for a young audience, familiar with the concept of mixed media, uninhibited by ideas of what theatre ought to be.

But to say this is also to simplify. For the Round House had become, primarily, the temple of the blown mind. The 'permissive' avant-garde groups, like the Living Theatre, had found a home there. Stop thinking, was the message. Shed your inhibitions, and let yourself go. . . .

But the strength of the Ardens' theatre has always been an ability to create physical excitement and, at the same time, keep a hold on the intelligence. The Ardens, like Brecht, think through the senses: but they don't surrender their intelligence to a river of uncontrollable emotion. In *The Hero Rises Up*, the intelligence is always there, commenting on the extravagance and the physical excitement.

The Ardens brought a sharp, political intelligence to the mind-blown hippies of the Round House. But the intelligence was largely lost in the technical defects of the situation. What blew the minds was Mark Boyle's light-show, which was stylistically irrelevant. The complexities of the Ardens' statement were very difficult to put across.

Simon Trussler's answer to this is that the Ardens should forget their experiments outside the 'legitimate' theatre and hand the show over to a professional director. But their experience, later, with the Nottingham Playhouse production in Edinburgh, hardly suggests that this is the solution. The text was cut: the Ardens felt that much of the political content had been removed, in spite of their objections: and the music was prettified out of existence. (At the Round House, Boris Haworth's home-made, mathematically programmed music, which included a violin with one string, and a steam-organ, was one of the delights.)

Trussler's argument implies that the Ardens are wilfully

rejecting professional theatre, and that they are committed to roughness, sloppiness and a vague, communal goodwill. The fact is that the professional theatre in this country has seldom been able to produce the 'style of entertainment' Arden's work demands – just as few professional groups in English theatre have ever captured the style of Brecht. At best, there have been good, individual performances: at worst, panto-mime has been reduced to a tepid, naturalistic joke, and plays have been emptied of the bawdy, slapstick and broad comedy that would give them real vitality. What Arden demands is the obscenity of a Frankie Howerd, the comic timing of old pros like Morecambe and Wise, the extrovert qualities of Hollywood stars, such as John Wayne and Richard Widmark. What he has usually been given is the intense, introvert straining after inner psychological truth that is at the heart of British drama teaching – and that is completely at odds with the style in which he is working.

The problem isn't Arden's alone. Not long ago, Henry Livings described to me how he'd tried to persuade an actor to play a scene in a chair hanging from the flies. 'It was a lovely chair,' Livings said. 'You moved to the right and you flew over there; you moved to the left, and back you came. It was great just swinging through the air. This fellow tried it a couple of times in rehearsal, and then said, "But I can't *act* in this." So I told him to forget it.'

Joan Littlewood has tried to solve the problem by creating her own companies. 'They're great when they're playing or improvising,' she said of one of her latest groups of actors, 'but when they get on the stage they will fucking *act*. They'll grow out of it.' But the financial pressures prevent her from achieving the continuity she needs.

It isn't, to my mind, surprising, that the Ardens, Joan Littlewood and Henry Livings are all, virtually, exiles from the British theatre. All of them belong to a comic tradition which has no place in the theatre establishment: and they belong to that tradition because the political attitude they instinctively take up has led them to a rejection of the values the legitimate British theatre still expresses.

In spite of the surface changes over the last fifteen years, the British theatre is still buried in a form that asserts that feelings are more important than actions, that intentions matter more than effects, and that appearances are to be equated with reality.

Faced with this situation, the avant-garde underground has been fighting mock-battles. Abandoning any attempts at genuine communication, they have assaulted the audience, have set up mindless, aggressive shock images, and have imagined they have been striking a blow for revolution by taking off their clothes and using four-letter words.

The problem facing Henry Livings, Joan Littlewood and the Ardens is that they don't belong either to the nineteenth-century hangover which is represented by the official theatre; or to the arty decadence of the avant-garde. They are solidly rooted in a popular tradition: and so they aren't taken seriously, either by the guardians of established culture, or by the non-thinking underground.

Joan Littlewood summed up the situation when she said, 'We can't go on making happenings with students at street-corners. Somebody, somewhere, has got to get down to creating serious, professional work.'

The Ardens are, at the moment, faced with the need to train a group capable of acting professionally in the style their work demands; and then to find an audience which is neither that of the Royal Court, prepared to slum emotionally over David Storey's miners, nor that of the pop world, demanding its cathartic shock. As Joan Littlewood's career has shown, nobody is prepared to give financial support for that kind of long-term exercise. The British theatre depends, ultimately, either on the solid, middle-class support it has always commanded; or on the droppings of a benevolent-minded Arts

Council which has its own ideas of what 'experimental theatre' ought to be.

John Arden is one of the greatest dramatists in the English language for several centuries. Lip service is paid to the occasional play – *Serjeant Musgrave's Dance*, or *Live Like Pigs*. But he is denied the conditions he needs for his work. In the late sixties and early seventies the only way in which he could work creatively was to write short plays for political demonstrations – or live in out-of-the-way rural localities, where he is, at least, dealing with a concrete and meaningful political situation.

It was out of this dilemma that, before leaving for India in 1969, John Arden created the most personal statement in dramatic terms that he has so far written. It was a radio play, and it was called *The Bagman*.

5

Portrait of the Artist as a Reprehensible Coward

The Bagman is a witty, precise, imaginative, and very painful statement about the state of mind Arden found himself in during 1969. It is a story told by a Narrator, who introduces himself in the opening sequence:

> John Arden (thirty-eight) of ancient family,
> Writer of plays for all the world to see,

> To see, and pay for, and to denigrate:
> Such was my work since 1958.

Arden scrutinizes himself through the eyes of this narrator:

> If, on this soggy Thursday, I should fall down dead,
> What of my life and death would then be said?
> 'He covered sheets of paper with his babble,
> He covered yards of stage-cloth with invented people,
> He worked alone for years yet was not able
> To chase one little rat from underneath the table.'

The narrator goes for a walk in Highgate Wood, and an old gypsy comes and offers him a bag for ten shillings. The last person who bought the bag, she says, found an 'elegant soft young woman' (an ironic comment on the concept of a poetic Muse). And since

> I was in a mood for fornication,
> And also I was, was I not, in a dream . . .

he buys the bag. But before he can unfasten it, he is chased out of the park by a keeper ('His pencil was enormous, stuck weapon-wise in his belt').

Outside, the narrator finds himself in a strange land. It is peopled by outlandish folk who are starving. They attack him, because they think there is food in his bag. But they are brutally beaten off by soldiers, who pick up the narrator and take him to a city.

The city is dirty and ill-kept – the narrator is kicked into a square where a kind of entertainment is going on. A Popular Minister presents a female dancer ('Give her a bit of a slap and tickle') and throws sweets to the crowd. The crowd fights over the sweets, because some of them are pearls. An Unpopular Minister appears and is booed – but he points to the stranger the horsemen have brought into the town. The narrator comments:

> It is not at all agreeable
> To be glared at by all the people.
> I do not hold that man to be wise
> Who desires to be made the cynosure of all eyes.

The Unpopular Minister calls the narrator on to the stage. 'Professor Inkspot is his name,' he says, and the crowd all sing:

> 'Professor Inkspot tell us now
> Why you walk like a pregnant sow . . .'

The scene is like a childhood nightmare. The narrator is ordered to open his bag. And so he does. And out of it tumble little men.

The narrator suddenly finds himself speaking in the voice of Adolf Hitler:

> My little people in a row
> Sit on the stage and watch the show.
> The show they watch is rows and rows
> Of people watching them. Who knows
> Which is more alive than which?

The little people put on a show. There is a Soldier-boy 'in coat of red' who

> Is every one of you whose head
> Is turned by dreams of power achieved
> Through violence and the tears of the bereaved . . .

a Constable 'so stiff and straight':

> Is any man who thinks that Right
> Must stamp on Wrong till Wrong can claim
> That Right was twice as much to blame.

and a 'bright-eyed Girl':

> She is any girl who will lie down,
> Whether for love or half-a-crown,

F

And rising up again, will say:
'That's enough then for today,
Do not expect as much tomorrow . . .'

The references to *Serjeant Musgrave's Dance* are clear, and
Arden adds:

The conclusion was ominous. Hacked and splintered wooden
limbs lay everywhere upon the platform, and of those mannikins
who were not dead only the most crippled and the weakest
seemed to have enough voice to bewail their ill-fortune and to
call upon the world for redress.

Arden is referring to the kind of theatre which expresses
moral indignation out of weakness. And he goes on to make a
direct comment on the theatrical effect of catharsis. 'None who
watched were able to restrain their tears. The more so because
all the time an unseen music had been ringing and clanging,
stirring the heart and turning the entrails of all that spell-
bound auditory. . . .'

The political situation Arden has shown is barbarous.
Outside, people are starving and nailed to trees; inside, they
are cheated by corrupt ministers. But the insiders have their
'revolutionary theatre'. 'Even the Unpopular Minister was
smiling.' 'Most impressive,' he says. 'Educational.' And the
Popular Minister adds, 'I have never known the people so
delighted, so enlivened, so thoroughly stimulated both
intellectually and emotionally as they have been this after-
noon.' In the meantime there are brigands to be executed.
'The Junior Magistrates will attend to the next business. . . .'

Arden is trying to examine objectively the effects of
'revolutionary theatre'. The Ministers, in *The Bagman*, discuss
the possible effects of the play they have seen: but, meanwhile,
outside the window, the crowd is screaming in delight at the
execution of the brigands. 'In my view,' says the Popular
Minister, 'the Professor is a young man to be encouraged:
though of course we must be careful.' 'We can encourage him

by all means,' replies the Unpopular Minister. 'And control him.' 'Not control,' says the Popular Minister. 'Suggest directions. . . .'

The narrator is put away in peace and quiet, and is sent a 'personal gratification' in the shape of a young girl. But now Arden puts the other side of the picture of 'revolutionary theatre'. For the play, which has not, apparently, affected the mass of the populace has stirred the girl to rebellion.

The girl explains to the narrator the economy of the city. The town's wealth is provided by 'selected men' who 'descend by ropes to dig and shovel'. They are digging treasure that has been left there by murderers – and these original murderers are the 'outlandish' men who are now shut out of the town. But the treasure the citizens think is theirs:

> . . . isn't theirs at all. There is a great King across the water who takes as much of it as he wants, provides the citizens with the food that ought to be being grown upon the farms of the out-landish men – if they had farms, which they once had – he deter-mines his own price for the treasure that is dug up – he has an ambassador in this town to supervise the diggings, and he appoints and pays and administers the horsemen who ride patrol. . . . Oh, the whole economy of this region is entirely ridiculous – you wouldn't credit it if you met it in real life: but then you are in a dream. . . .

Arden is again using a Brechtian technique of alienation. He describes in childlike terms a situation we all recognize as our own – and shows it to be strange and absurd.

The young woman, whose father had been 'outlandish', has been stirred up by the narrator's little men. 'You send us more remembrances like that, little man, there will be no protection left, no security, no good dinners, nothing but the truth.' 'I wished I was back in Muswell Hill,' comments the narrator: but instead, he finds himself confronted by the Ambassador of the great king across the water, 'a great big man with a face like a bucket of blood', who is eating seven eggs at once.

The Ambassador comments on his work:

> You set afoot unauthorized imitations of people you should despise and you blow them out like bullfrogs with the imagination of their strength. *At* the same time, however, you reserve to yourself a sharp pin with which you can at your own convenience prick their distended bellies and explode them into nothing. The first part of your programme, from my point of view, is abhorrent. From the point of view of the underdog people to whom you address yourself, the second part is likewise. Therefore, you are very bold, and a man to be objectively admired: or else you are a hedger, and a fencesitter, and a contemptible poltroon. I wonder which?

The statement is a very sharp comment on Arden's own work. Arden is asking questions of himself. In the *Peace News* interview about *The Workhouse Donkey* he had denied Wesker's description of him as a 'wishy-washy liberal'. A liberal, he said, was a person who put both sides of the argument because he was committed to neither: he, on the other hand, was committed to *understanding* both sides, no matter which side he temperamentally favoured.[1] Arden uses the Ambassador to comment on criticisms that other people have made about him.

The Ambassador throws eggs at him, and the yolk dribbles down his chest. He is then led into a 'gallery full of male and female dragonflies'. He is in the presence of the King and the Queen, and they order him to open his bag.

The narrator makes the same speech as the one he has made before:

> But I felt less at ease than on the previous occasion . . . now, If I was Hitler, it was Hitler in the Berlin bunker of 1945, and the boots of the Red Army were stamping above my head.

[1] *Peace News* interview—see page 25 footnote (in *Encore* p. 16).

And there is no fighting or revolution in this story:

> They were not even the same sort of people as before. . . .
> Nothing but extraordinary variations of erotic postures and
> intrigues, couplings and triplings and quadruplings . . . while
> the audience muttered and laughed and clapped a little and
> conversed one with another . . . The music was erotic also, but
> more than a little insipid. . . .

If the first play out of the bag contained references to
Serjeant Musgrave's Dance, this belongs to the world of *Oh!
Calcutta!*, a theatre which has replaced revolution by erotic
titillation. It is a theatre which is acceptable to the establishment. 'It was quite a relief,' says the King, 'to hear the – hear
the truth about ourselves'; and the Queen adds delightedly,
'Yes, it made us squirm.'

The narrator is kept in luxury in the palace, on condition
that he keeps on repeating the performance. 'It was all very
indolent and agreeable, and very much beside the point.'
But at this moment, he is awakened again by the girl: 'Within
your dream you fell asleep again.' His success at court has
been a fantasy – all that is real is the yolk from the Ambassador's eggs.

The narrator finds himself, not at court, but in a rubbish
dump, with the true king, 'Chained to the wall'; and he is
being pursued by the guards. The girl drags him down into a
sewer, where a group of wild men with axes are waiting. The
girl introduces the narrator as their brother, and they tell him
to throw down his bag and take up a weapon. 'This *is* my
weapon,' cries the narrator, and he opens his bag.

But the little men refuse to come out. They cry:

> Men of war do not require
> To see themselves in a truthful mirror
> All that they need to spur them to action
> Is their own most bloody reflection
> In the white eyeballs of their foe. . . .

> Please let us please let us get back into the sack.
> When the battle has been won
> We can peep out again and creep back.

While the rebels are watching 'this fool with his bag', the soldiers arrive, 'And in an instant all was blood and death and furious weapons swung at random in the dark'. The narrator falls beneath a stamping foot – and then awakes, to find himself on Highgate Underground Station. As he is leaving the station he sees the woman who had sold him the bag. She is selling white heather, and she says to him:

> You did not find what you expected
> What you found you did not use
> What you saw you did not look at
> When you looked at it you would not choose!

The narrator replies:

> It would have been easy, it would have been good
> To have carried a bag full of solid food
> And fed the thin men till they were
> As fat as the men who held them in fear
> But such is not the nature of these bags
> That are given away by old women in rags.
> Such is not my nature, nor will be.
> All I can do is to look at what I see . . .

The irony of the narrator's final speech is unmistakable. Except to the BBC Head of Drama, Martin Esslin, who saw the play as Arden's farewell to political commitment. The speech is cool and detached – but the detachment only makes Arden's criticism of the narrator's attitude all the more pointed.

The lines express the resigned shrug of the liberal intellectual confronted by an unjust world he feels himself powerless to change. Outside the city, men are starved and nailed to trees; inside the rich manipulate the poor; in the sewer, all is blood and death. Oh, dear, says the 'artist': I suppose it would have been nice to do something about it. Still, that's not my nature; that's not what I'm good at: that's not what my muse is about. 'All I can do is to look at what I see.'

The speech pinpoints the nature of the confusion about Arden's work. For if the actor identifies with the character – makes the speech 'sincere' – he'll try to carry the audience along with the apology. And the response will be, 'Poor man! What a dilemma! But how honest!'

But if the actor stands outside the character, comments with his voice on the outrageousness of what is being said, communicates satirically the resigned complacency of the narrator's attitude – as an Adrian Mitchell poem puts it: 'You said: there is nothing I can do. As you said it you seemed so proud'[1] – then Arden's meaning becomes the precise opposite of a 'farewell to commitment'.

The Bagman is, in fact, an ironic, intelligent, funny and bitterly serious critique of a cultural position: of the position that it's possible, in the present barbarous and unjust state of the world, to make art that is neutral, uncommitted, objective. The fact that the man in the play who defends that position is called 'John Arden' is one more of Arden's paradoxes. It enables him to make the focus clear and sharp.

In 1959, near the beginning of Arden's career, critics identified with Serjeant Musgrave – and found *Serjeant Musgrave's Dance* confusing. Eleven years later, Martin Esslin identified with the 'John Arden' of *The Bagman* and saw an ironic political statement as a piece of subjective self-exploration.

The ultimate irony is that at the precise moment when Esslin was announcing Arden's farewell to politics, the Ardens were in India, where they found themselves drawn towards a revolutionary political movement – and, briefly, held in jail. They returned from India with a much sharper awareness of the need for political action, and an even greater sense of alienation from established western cultural values.

[1] 'Loose Leaf Poem', *Ride the Nightmare*, Cape 1971, p. 96.

The first concrete product of this awareness was a new play, written in Ireland in 1972, and first produced, not in the West End, but in a college in Falls Road in Belfast.

The play – the Ardens' first piece for the theatre since *The Hero Rises Up* – is called *The Ballygombeen Bequest*.

6

The Ballygombeen Bequest

The Ballygombeen Bequest tells the story of an English absentee landlord and his relationship with a family which lives in a cottage on the estate he has inherited in Ireland. The estate consists of the cottage and a bungalow. The landlord, Lt-Col Holliday-Cheype, uses the bungalow as a holiday home for rich tourists, and the O'Leary family act as unpaid caretakers. Eventually, he swindles them out of any rights they may have had to the cottage the family has lived in for more than a century, and, when the husband, Seamus, grows too old to be useful, orders the family to leave, intending to sell the whole property to a development company. When the son, Padraic, tries to organize resistance, the Official IRA offers help. With the help of a local contractor, Hagan, they blow up the bungalow. But a British intelligence agent, tipped off by Holliday-Cheype, and an agent of the Dublin Special Branch bait a trap for Padraic. They persuade him to go north of the border to sell ponies, and there he's arrested by the British army. He dies under questioning and is dumped back across the border, where his death is attributed to internecine strife between branches of the IRA. But in the meantime, Hagan, the contractor, has pointed out to Holliday-Cheype that nobody's going to buy his property now that the IRA has put its mark on it. Hagan gets the property cheap, while the English landlord says he'll move on to Europe to see what pickings there are there.

The first point to make about *The Ballygombeen Bequest* is that it's the first of the Ardens' plays to take up a clear-cut Marxist position. Not that the Ardens' Marxism is abstract or theoretical. It has arisen directly out of their experiences in India. Soon after his return from India, Arden said, in a lecture at Bradford University, that whenever he wrote anything in future, he would be asking himself how it would look through the eyes of an Indian revolutionary. In *The Ballygombeen Bequest*, the Ardens successfully relate one local incident in an isolated corner of Ireland to a Marxist world-view. In the middle of the play, the Narrator sings a song, to the tune of 'John Barleycorn':

> From nineteen-fifty-seven
> To nineteen-sixty-eight
> The fat men of the fat half-world
> Had food on every plate.
> The lean men of the naked world
> Grew leaner every day
> And if they put their faces up
> Their teeth were kicked away . . .
> And if in narrow holes they crouched
> Defences to contrive,
> They were spread with flaming jelly
> Till not one was left alive.
> For the fat men at their dinner-board
> Could never bear to think
> That creeping fingers from below
> Might steal their meat and drink.

The Ardens see the world as divided into those who have, and those who have not. Those who have continually get more: those who have not get less and less. The only way they will save themselves is by taking, forcibly if necessary, from those who have. Padraic, the O'Leary son, has learnt this in a building strike at Manchester. His message is, 'Educate, Agitate . . . Organize'.

But if the world-picture is Marxist, the Ardens' style remains music-hall. The play is very funny. Holliday-Cheype is a character in the Dr Copperthwaite tradition. He has the same kind of patter and conscienceless bonhomie. There's a hilarious scene in which his lawyer coaches him in the writing of a letter to the O'Learys. The letter is complaining that they've been slacking and threatening them with punishment – and is also saying that their usual gratuity is being withheld. Holliday-Cheype makes it sound like a greetings card.

Again, there are the usual Arden 'play-within-a-play' devices, the juggling with levels of reality. So, the O'Leary family does an old family retainer act with Holliday-Cheype, and Holliday-Cheype at one time himself orders the singing narrator to confine his caterwauling to the narrative. The play is sprinkled with asides to the audience, songs and music – all the devices of the popular tradition.

And there are a number of rich caricatures – in particular one of a British secret agent, who is disguised as a documentary film-maker, making picturesque films about the beauties of nature for the BBC and the art circuit. He films Padraic's sister with flowers round her neck – but takes good care that Padraic himself will be in the picture, so that later he can be kept in secret service files.

But the most successful pantomime device is kept until the end. After a scene in which Padraic has died under questioning, and after the funeral, the Ardens end the play with a custard-pie fight. The custard-pies are thrown at each other by Holliday-Cheype and the contractor, Hagan – a farcical image of the conflicts between the exploiters. And, as Holliday-Cheype announces his departure for Europe, the dead Padraic puts a custard-pie under the landlord's feet. Holliday-Cheype ends the play sprawling.

These popular dramatic devices are used to present and explain a very complex situation. For if the world-view of the play is simple, the detailed analysis – the way in which the Ardens show the tangled structures of Irish society – is both subtle and masterly. The Ardens start from a clear-cut position. It's a position that is so clear-cut that the normal explanation that the British army is in Ulster to protect Catholics from Protestants can, by the time it's stated, be greeted with incredulous laughter. But the Ardens don't simply make an assertion, assume that it's self-evidently right, and leave it at that. As much as in the earlier plays they take care to show everybody's motives, to explain the reasons behind everyone's actions. Holliday-Cheype is out to make money. From his point of view, the O'Learys are, at first, useful, but later a nuisance. Hagan, too, is out to make money: by the end of the play we see precisely why he's willing to sign the O'Learys' petition, put Padraic in touch with the IRA, and even blow up the bungalow himself, for the IRA. His motives have nothing to do with social revolution. The Ardens show how the IRA itself can be used by the exploiters.

Again, the British secret agent is concerned with law and order. To him, Padraic is an agitator who will extend the troubles from Northern Ireland to the South. And so, there's an alliance between him and his opposite number from Dublin. Even the Corporal who arrests Padraic is given his reasons. 'I'm what they call a mercenary,' he says. 'Then you ought to be ashamed,' says Padraic; and the Corporal replies, 'For what? For earning wages to keep a wife and three kids in Scunthorpe and like-as-not make her a widow because you bloody Irish have all gone mad? You find me a good job in England, boy, I tell you I'd never have set foot. . . .'

The Ardens aren't primarily concerned with asserting rights and wrongs. They're concerned with the *how*. *How* does exploitation work; *how* is the Dublin establishment linked with the Ulster establishment and the English establishment in preserving the *status quo*? *How* are the interests, of those who have, interlocked against those who have not? *The Ballygombeen Bequest* offers, in the form of a popular entertainment, a model of an unjust society.

But perhaps the most important point about this play is the context from which it grew. Since their return from India the Ardens have been living in a country area in the west of Ireland. They have worked there with some of the local inhabitants, making, for example, a film about Oughterard and the threat to turn it into a tourist paradise.

The Ballygombeen Bequest was first produced in the Falls Road, Belfast, at the height of the conflict there. This was theatre *in* a political situation used not for repeating familiar propaganda slogans, but for teaching people, through entertainment, to understand more clearly the complexities and contradictions and underlying realities of their own situation.

With *The Ballygombeen Bequest* the Ardens have moved into a new dimension of political theatre. But they have done so while retaining all the elements of wit, gaiety and playfulness that have always been at the heart of their work together – and also at the heart of all John Arden's plays.

Postscript December 1972:
The Island of the Mighty

Since the rest of this book was written, the Ardens have made a controversial return to the London theatre. In December 1972 the Royal Shakespeare Company presented a new Arden/D'Arcy play, *The Island of the Mighty*, at the Aldwych. The story of the production illustrates the thesis of this book – that the revolutionary content of Arden's plays makes stylistic demands that are outside the normal range of the established British theatre.

The Island of the Mighty is not so much a new play as a revised version of three old ones. It was originally conceived in 1966 as a trilogy for BBC television: but the policy of the BBC Drama Department was changed and the project was shelved. Arden then re-shaped the play for a theatre company in Wales. The result was a much longer play than the original television trilogy. It proved to be beyond the resources of the Welsh company.

This extended script then went the rounds of the London theatre managements, but was left unpresented for three years. Then, in 1972, the Royal Shakespeare Company decided to stage the play, but asked Arden for a drastically shortened version. He and Margaretta D'Arcy re-wrote the play together.

Both the time-lag, and the fact that the new version was the result of a collaboration, are important. The original play had been written before the Ardens' visit to India: the revised version took account of what they had seen there. And the original play had sprung largely from John Arden's literary and historical preoccupations – he had taken the religious myths of the period as a major theme. Whereas now, he and Margaretta D'Arcy shifted the emphasis towards the economic breakdown of a tribal society, drawing, in the process, on their observations of India.

Arden explains what they were about in an article in *Flourish* – the RSC news-sheet.

> National myths of this sort present a picture of a way of life similar to that which today exists in the Third World. . . . The Third World of our own day will find its own Homers from among its own people. We have attempted no more than to indicate – from a rocking and sinking and post-Imperial standpoint . . . – something of how the early history of Britain foreshadows twentieth-century turbulence. 'Kynge Arthur is nat dede' – but he seems to have changed sides. The true voice of liberty is more likely to be heard today from the kind of men and women who have little part to play in the traditional tales: I mean the ones who did the work, who fed and housed the noble warriors, and equipped them for their fight.

The Ardens' standpoint, in fact, is that of Brecht in his poem, *Questions of a Working Man* ('On the night the Chinese wall was finished / Where did the masons go?'). What the Ardens tried to do, in revising the play, was to set the traditional heroic events firmly inside the framework of an oppressive social system. King Arthur and his followers ('the tattered dragon and his brood') go through their motions of heroism and chivalry against a background of peasant suffering and poverty. Their gestures need to be seen continually against this background.

This framework clearly affects the style of the performance. Without the background of the peasants, the play can be interpreted as telling the tragic story of a once great king in decline. The emphasis will then be on the pathos of an ageing hero. But, set against the peasant background, Arthur becomes a ludicrous, posturing figure. He demands to be presented with irony.

In the RSC production, the irony was missing. Michael Billington, in *The Guardian*, praised Patrick Allen for capturing Arthur's pathos – which was, presumably, one of the reasons why the Ardens felt the meaning of their play had been distorted. And with the irony much of the fun had disappeared. Gags which should have been light and quick were slow and laboured. Actors asked to chase each other round the stage with the zany speed of Keystone cops trundled round like overweight elephants. Sword fights that should have had the abstract comic quality of Chinese opera looked like amateur costume drama. And in place of this lightness and speed the RSC company offered a post-Stanislavski concentration on inner motivation, a grasping for intensity of feeling. The extrovert, circus-like quality of the Ardens' script was turned into an introvert meditation about the decline of a kingdom.

In the absence of an adequate production, the play can only be judged as a written text. As such it is impressive, and contains two of the most powerful images the Ardens have invented: the image of the lame King; and the image of Merlin, the court poet, who in the end takes on the role of a bird.

The lame King is Arthur himself. He is physically lame, and his verbal rhetoric is always set off ironically against the physical fact that he hobbles about the stage. Patrick Allen made this hobbling pathetic: to this has old age reduced a once-great King. But the lameness in the text is clearly intended as a comic image of the hollowness of Arthur's glory. The image is echoed in the story of Balan and Balin on the island. Balan has been taken to the island by a Princess, has fought and killed a lame King, and then wakes from a drunken sleep to find himself lame. He will remain King for a year, until a new King comes to kill *him*. (The new King turns out to be his brother, Balin, in a mask – and he has come long before the year has run out. The brothers kill each other.)

The legend is, of course, well known, but the Ardens use it as an image of the ultimate powerlessness of authority. 'These people have ill customs,' says Balan before he dies. The poet adds: 'We make our King lame so that he cannot escape'. He must live here in his luxury until a stronger King overthrows him. The dying Balin says to the Queen: 'I think it is the Roman horsemen who will come to trample you down. But I saw them, they are such old men strapped up with hooks of iron.'

These lines at the end of the scene bring us back directly to Arthur himself. The Ardens use the image of lameness to demonstrate one of the play's main themes: that those who seek imperial power may achieve it, but will be themselves crippled in the process.

The figure of Merlin is very complex. He is related in some ways to the courtly poet of *Armstrong's Last Goodnight*, that is to say, he is urbane, intelligent, clever, well-intentioned, self-critical. But he has allowed himself to be used by what he calls 'the wolf-pack' – King Arthur and his army. And when he is finally called on to act, he fails, and goes on to retreat into his private madness, living in the forests as an isolated bird. In their portrait of Merlin, the Ardens' irony is clear and sharp: in the RSC production, the figure was turned into something approaching camp.

What the whole story of the RSC production did, in fact, highlight was the gap between the Ardens' ways of working and the methods of an established professional company. To the Ardens the quarrel was, first and foremost, about basic rights. They were, they insisted, members of the Society of Irish Playwrights, which was affiliated to Irish Equity, and as such they claimed that clauses in their contract were not being honoured. It was, they say, the RSC's refusal to negotiate with them over these rights which led them to picket the theatre.

But the reason why they felt their rights had been affected was that, when Margaretta D'Arcy saw the first run-through,

about ten days before the first preview, she felt that the
meaning of the play was being distorted. In an interview in
Time Out, David Jones made much of the fact that Margaretta
D'Arcy's intervention had come so late. But what he did not
say was that it had previously been agreed, with his approval,
that she should not attend earlier rehearsals, since it was felt
that she should be in a position to bring a fresh eye to the first
run-through – which would still leave time for necessary
changes. In fact Arden had already expressed doubts about
the direction the production was taking, but had been asked
in a formal fashion by David Jones not to interfere but to
wait until the run-through. (See *Author's note* below.)

After the run-through, the Ardens expressed disapproval
of several aspects of the production, including set, costumes
and music. But they realized that it was too late to change the
songs and the setting, and therefore wanted merely to discuss
ways of making the play's meaning more clear. But at this
point it became clear that the changes were not going to be
made, and that there was nothing the Ardens could do about
it.

After the argument broke, some of the actors asked the
Ardens to set up a discussion. Later, however, after David
Jones had warned them that discussion so near to opening
night might only confuse the actors and thus lead to a first-
night disaster, the actors themselves voted against such a discussion, and that was the end of it.

The Ardens argue that all their rows in the theatre have
been about conditions of work for the playwright. The
Aldwych dispute, they say, demonstrates that the standard
playwrights' contract is full of loopholes, and that authors
have no rights at all when it comes to the crunch.

But the crunch came because the Ardens and the RSC
management were looking at theatre from completely different
directions. How remote David Jones is from understanding
the basic implications of the Ardens' work in theatre is

demonstrated, first of all, by the letter he and Trevor Nunn wrote to *The Times*, describing the RSC as 'a left-wing theatre'; and, secondly, by the attitude to political theatre he revealed in an article in *Theatre Quarterly*, in which he described his methods of rehearsal in Günter Grass's *The Plebeians Rehearse the Uprising*. Finding that his actors were politically conservative, and that they knew nothing about Marxism, he organized, he says, classes in Marxism, in which the actors read round and discussed passages from Marx. After some weeks of this, he presented them with a speech by Willy Brandt – and they immediately described it as reactionary.

In other words, David Jones believes that a few discussion groups had been enough to educate his actors to play in 'left-wing theatre'. With these discussions behind them they could, presumably, feel competent to tackle a play which criticized a playwright (Bertolt Brecht) who had spent his whole life putting together a theory of theatre, and years of his life creating a collective of actors who could understand, work with, and change that theory in practice.

The Ardens, in their search for new, collective working methods, are closer to Brecht than they are to the British theatre establishment: not because they are 'Marxist' or 'left-wing', but because they have consistently produced work which cannot be squeezed into the conventions of 'legitimate' theatre, and because the nature of this work has driven them unceasingly to find alternative solutions.

The Island of the Mighty, as Arden himself said before the controversy with the RSC had developed, belongs with the earlier plays for the professional theatre, rather than with the more recent plays that have been put together outside the established framework. He cannot, he says, see himself writing more plays in that genre. The plays he intends to write with Margaretta D'Arcy in the future will, he says, be different.

Just how different they'll be they won't know till they've written them.

Author's Note

Arden's version of what was happening during the rehearsals was confirmed by my own experience. About six weeks before the run-through, I sat in on a day's rehearsal. Arden was there, mainly in order to make any changes in the text that seemed to be necessary, and to agree these with director and actors.

The rehearsal process seemed to me to be all wrong. The play demanded a group approach, based on collectively worked-out gags, physical activity and lots of extrovert games. Instead, what happened was that the director would discuss privately, and at some length, with individual actors the interpretation of their lines. The actors were hugging their parts to themselves, resisting when any of their lines were cut, working at creating psychologically convincing characters.

Over lunch, I talked to Arden about the rehearsal process. He told me that it had been agreed that Margaretta D'Arcy should stay away until the run-through, while he worked on the detail of the text, so that she could come in and see the whole from outside and judge how the play was reading, a difficult thing to do when you've been immersed in the separate details. This seemed to me to be a very good idea: she had done exactly this when I'd produced *The Happy Haven* with a student group, and her intervention had been very helpful.

I asked Arden if he shared my doubts about the way the production was going. He said he did: and that he had discussed the question with David Jones. He had explained to David Jones exactly what he wanted. In return, David Jones had explained that he understood the Ardens' intentions, and that he was going to carry them out; but that these actors had been trained to work in a particular way, and that to change their working methods at this stage would only confuse them. They would eventually arrive at the extrovert performance the Ardens' wanted, but they had to be allowed to reach it in their own way. And Arden added, 'After all, I'm not a director. All I can do is make my intentions clear and trust the director to get there in the end.' By the time of the run-through, it was clear that the production had not got there in the end; and that nothing either of the Ardens said at that stage was going to make any difference.

Appendix A:
John Arden and Peter Brook

One of the most interesting productions of an Arden play was Peter Brook's version, in 1963, of *Serjeant Musgrave's Dance*, in Paris, in French. Like all Peter Brook's work, it was theatrically brilliant: but it helped to illuminate some of the differences between Arden and the theatrical avant-garde.

Brook's approach to the play was made more difficult by the French translation. Although Arden himself supervised the translation, and it was, literally, very accurate, it proved impossible to translate into French the rich, colloquial, essentially northern flavour of Arden's language. The words were there: the associations conjured up by the words weren't. For example, when, in the English version, the Bargee looks at Musgrave and sings, 'Here we sit like birds in the wilderness . . .' the song, traditional, belongs to a whole known world of reference. But when, in the French version, the Bargee sang, to no particular tune, 'Nous sommes deux oiseaux', an evocative song had been turned into a simple literary metaphor.

This literariness tended to take over throughout the whole play. 'The action is the argument,' Arden had said about his work: but here the argument became a verbal one, words in the mouths of characters expressing a point of view. The tradition was that of Sartre and Camus, rather than that of the English popular theatre.

Brook's production tended to emphasize this 'intellectual'

quality. He set out to create, not so much a popular story built around familiar associations, as a generalized nightmare.

For example, one of the central images of the play is the 'blood-red rose'. In his opening speech, the Bargee gives this name to the soldiers, because they used to be beaten until their backs were red. But the image relates to what we can *see* on the stage – soldiers in scarlet uniforms. At the end of the play, we're given a true image of a soldier – a white skeleton in red rags.

Peter Brook's production, however, was built around a grey-green motif. In the opening scene, the soldiers were dressed in blue-grey overcoats; and what dominated the stage was the slab on which Sparky stood. This was a grey-green abstraction, which was used throughout the play. In the graveyard scene, for example, it broke up to give a vague, semi-abstract impression of tombstones, blurring the imagery of the original scene, which was built round black, red and white. And it formed the partition between the beds in the scene in which Annie goes from soldier to soldier, until she finds, in Sparky, one as lost and as human as herself.

This scene, in particular, emphasized the way in which Brook, striving for dramatic effect, muddied the clarity of the play. In the original, it has the quality of a folk tale. An action is repeated, with variations, three times. In Brook's version, this rhythm was broken. Sparky was picked out from the start: he slept, not in a box, like the others, but apart, and under the stairs. More important, Musgrave, who ought visually to be part of the scene – he sleeps in a bed on a raised platform and seems to dominate the others, who call him God, even in his sleep – was tucked away high in a box amongst the audience. This was a formalist attempt to break out of the proscenium arch, and it made for a startling dramatic effect. A voice suddenly came from on high. But the *visual* counterpoint between Musgrave's law and order, and

Sparky's fearful decision to accept 'life and love', was completely lost.

It was, though, at the end that Brook most seriously violated Arden's original. Arden has made his intentions quite clear. Musgrave has tried to break the circle of violence and counter-violence, but he has failed, and the circle has reformed, *visually*, on the stage, as miners and dragoons (black overwhelmed by scarlet) dance round Annie who is nursing the white-draped-with-scarlet skeleton of her lover. The dancers take up the Bargee's song of 'Finnegan, begin agen'. And it is after this that Attercliffe breaks the circle, when, left alone with Musgrave, he sings his song about the apple that holds a seed.

Brook staged this ending in such a way as to produce exactly the opposite effect. Attercliffe and Musgrave crouched under a grey-green platform, which had been turned into a prison, and Attercliffe sang his song, as dragoons and miners mimed a dance in the shadowy background. But as Attercliffe's song finished, the miners suddenly erupted on to the front of the stage, singing, 'Finnegan, begin agen'. So that it was with *this* image, and not with the image of the fallen seed and the raised orchard, that the play ended.

Brook had turned Arden's popular ballad into a statement of mid-century despair – the image of a nightmare that nobody can control.

In doing so, he had created a brilliant theatrical experience – but had lost the point of the play.

Appendix B: Working with Students on Arden Plays

By far the best way of finding out what Arden is about is to stop treating him as the author of literary texts, and work on the concrete presentation of his work. In 1964 I worked with a group of students from Shrewsbury School of Art on *Ars Longa, Vita Brevis* (the Ardens were at the same time working on the play with a group of Girl Guides at Kirbymoorside); and a year later, after having worked for a week with the Ardens in Ireland on the short play, *Friday's Hiding*, the same group presented a version of *The Happy Haven*. Both productions affected the way all those involved worked for many years after.

We began *Ars Longa, Vita Brevis* by playing games. There were eight in the group, aged eighteen upwards, and for several weeks we played children's games with the intensity that children themselves bring to their play. We played blind-man's buff, leapfrog, British bulldog, hide-and-seek games. We covered each other with scratches and bruises, but in the process discovered reserves of physical energy that we didn't know we possessed – and that eventually went into the production.

One or two of the games went directly into the production. For example, there's a game in which one person faces the wall, while the rest have to change position behind his back, without their movements being seen. The person who's 'on' turns round, trying to catch the others moving.

We translated this game into a classroom situation.

Miltiades, the art master, was loaded with cubes and boxes, which he kept arranging for the children to draw. Every time he turned to fuss with his boxes, with his back to the children, the children changed chairs: so that when he turned back they were always sitting in different positions. You felt the art master's grasp on reality was slipping, particularly since the 'children' were wearing masks the students had made, consisting simply of bare oblongs of cardboard, with round holes cut in for eyes. The masks gave the children a frightening, depersonalized effect. They looked at him with the distant knowingness of birds. Quite by accident, the scene had developed a typical Arden paradox: the authoritative schoolmaster had become the figure of fun whose grip of the situation was slack: the 'anarchist' children had become silent, frightening figures behind the uniform masks. . . .

The scene arose quite spontaneously – and this feeling of joyful spontaneity ran through all the work. One morning, two girls in a liberal studies music lesson made grotesque masks. When I looked at them, I said they'd got too much detail on them to work – but when we put them on they did work. They were very crude and home-made in quality – but their very crudity made them frightening. When we played the children's games wearing these masks, the quality of the games changed. They became emotionally very animal and violent. Once, during the Headmaster's opening speech, all the governors, wearing these masks, broke out into soulless, hysterical laughter. It was one of the most violent bits of theatre I've ever seen, but proved difficult to reproduce in performance.

Two of the scenes in particular were difficult to make work. One was the scene in which the art master, who has just been sacked, comes home to take tea with his wife. The dialogue is very formalized – Arden later said we should have thrown it away and improvised our own. But eventually we made the scene work by playing a game throughout the dialogue. The game was that the wife was trying to seduce the husband, while the husband was trying to build an abstract sculpture with his squares and triangles and cubes. Eventually, the art master ended up lying on the floor with his boxes, which the wife had kicked over, scattered around him. As he looked up from the rubble, he shouted, 'Have I not always been in command? Have I not always been able to control?' And the wife, flinging herself on top of him cried, 'My God, you are a Prussian.'

The other scene we couldn't make work was the final one, in which the wife, now a widow, celebrates her husband's death by enjoying herself 'in fast cars with innumerable young men, all more handsome and less confused than her late husband'. The scene, the Ardens had explained, ought to have a feeling of orgy about it. But it's hard to create a spontaneous celebration on a stage – and the Ardens, too, had difficulty making their orgy with the Girl Guides.

In *Ars Longa, Vita Brevis*, we created a number of wild, anarchic images – but when the Ardens saw our first performance, they commented that we'd lost the simplicity of the story-line, and the audience was confused. We'd had, for example, a man in a scarlet coat in the opening scene, and then the scarlet coat had reappeared, worn by someone else, in the final scene. We hadn't realized that the scarlet coat became in itself a striking image, even though all the characters wore masks, and people were asking what it was about. Later we worked hard on keeping the richness of texture while clarifying the narrative: and when, a year later, we came to work on *The Happy Haven*, we went above all for a clear story-line.

We began working on *The Happy Haven* in the same way we'd worked on *Ars Longa* – with games and improvisations. Because Copperthwaite, in his opening speech, describes the old people as if they were cars, we played with a lot of scenes in which cars were people and people were cars. Later we improvised the story-line of each scene, gradually coming back to the written text. (We found, in fact, that the writing is so dense and controlled that every line is important and pushes the story forward.)

We used the same approach to costume, props and masks that we'd used in *Ars Longa*. The costumes were anything we could find in the wardrobes of local dramatic societies, or in junk shops. The props were huge cardboard cut-outs – for example, for the scene in which the liquid turns green, we simply had a cut-out two-dimensional card, in the shape of a decanter, with the liquid painted brown on one side, green on the other. The moment of the greatest discovery in human history became a very obvious showman's trick. Mrs Phineus's birthday cake, in the opening scene, was also a cardboard cut-out. And in the scene in which Mrs Letouzel swindles Mrs Phineus out of her money, Mrs Letouzel (who was played by a boy) had an enormous bag, with huge envelopes, a huge pen, and a huge collecting box. As she produced each of these objects, the action of producing them became a gag in its own right.

The masks were designed with the help of the Ardens, and they went much further in exaggeration than the masks used in either the original Bristol or Royal Court productions. For example, Crape, the one who snoops around, had a huge nose; Golightly had the sad face of a clown.

The Ardens came to an early rehearsal, and said at once that the students were playing too hard at being old people. The action and the cues were slow, and the actors were dragging around the stage. Arden stressed the importance of an acrobatic performance. After that, we worked for frenetic pace, and the production became transformed. Crape leapt acrobatically from a high platform as he shouted, 'Because we're old, that's why . . .' the scene of the medical check-up became like an old film, played faster and faster, the old people whooped and chased each other round the stage.

A fortnight before the first performance, I still felt that something was missing. Margaretta D'Arcy saw some of our final rehearsals and pointed out that the final act should be played like a grotesque military operation – an old people's revolution. We began to accompany the action with the Marseillaise on the piano – and this gave a clue to what was missing. In music-hall there's always music. We were playing each scene as a music-hall turn: and so we invented signature tunes for all the leading characters. Whenever Copperthwaite entered, the piano played, 'Happy days are here again . . .' Golightly's tune was 'The man on the flying trapeze. . . .'

The whole final production was gay and farcical and anarchic: and made all the more startling a young girl's very direct and straight delivery of Mrs Phineus's 'old, old lady' speech near the end. The final seriousness of the play emerged through the fun. To all of us, it was a very satisfying experience.

Bibliographical Note

(a) PLAYS BY JOHN ARDEN

Serjeant Musgrave's Dance. London: Methuen, 1960.
The Workhouse Donkey. London: Methuen, 1964.
Armstrong's Last Goodnight. London: Methuen, 1965.
Left-Handed Liberty. London: Methuen, 1965.
Ironhand (adapted from Goethe's *Goetz von Berlichingen*).
    London: Methuen, 1965.
Soldier, Soldier and other plays (including *Soldier, Soldier, Friday's
    Hiding, When is a Door not a Door?* and *Wet Fish*). London:
    Methuen, 1967.
Three Plays (including *The Waters of Babylon, Live Like Pigs*
    and *The Happy Haven*). London: Penguin, 1969.
Two Autobiographical Plays (including *The Bagman* and *The
    True History of Squire Jonathan and His Unfortunate Treasure*).
    London: Methuen, 1971.

(b) PLAYS BY JOHN ARDEN AND
    MARGARETTA D'ARCY

The Business of Good Government. London: Methuen, 1963.
The Royal Pardon. London: Methuen, 1967.
The Hero Rises Up. London: Methuen, 1969.
Friday's Hiding. (Published in *Soldier, Soldier and other plays*.
    London: Methuen, 1967.
Ars Longa, Vita Brevis

Index